Terminal Diary 1918

Terminal Diary 1918

WWI at the Front

John Locke Doggett Jr

Gabrielle Barbour

Valor House

CONTENTS

CONTENTS

JOHN LOCKE DOGGETT JR

Coast Artillary Corps Officers order to France to report to Commanding General
Expeditionary Forces per Par 9 Conf O. 124 Designated by (x) and Par 2 Conf O. 126 designated
by (Y) Port of Embarkation

No.	Family Name followed by Christian	Rank	Regt Corps Det.	Notify in case of emergency	Rela- tion- ship	Address Number City State.
1	Mellon Albert R. (Y)	Capt	CARC	Mrs. J. A. Mellon	Mother	214 Hyde Park?1 Tampa, Fla.
2	Kessler Edward Z.(x)	1stLt	CAC	R. L. Kessler	Father	Charlotte, N.C.
3	Lamb Robert M.	"	(Prov) "	Charles T. Lamb	"	West Boylston, Mass
4	Little Edward R. (X)	"	CARC	R. T. Little	Mother	267 Main St. Brunswick, Me
5	Tenney Frank C. (X)	"	"	William M Tenney	Father	65 BrookmsideAve Jamaica Plains, Mass.
6	Thompson Harry T.(X)	"	"	Frank M. Thompson	Uncle	206 Bailey Ave. Chattanooga,Tenn
7	Walter Loyd D. (Y)	"	"	Adam Walter	Father	Oxford, Neb.
8	Doggett John L. (X)	2ndLt	CAC Prov.	J.L.Doggett	"	1121 Hurd Bldg. Jacksonville,Fla
9	Emerson William A.(X)	"	"	W. H. Emerson	"	160 W. North Ave Atlanta, Ga.
10	Cahill Ralph H. (Y)	"	CARC	Chas A Cahill,Mr.	"	683 Farewell Ave Milwaukee, Wisc.
11	Carmichael A.B. (Y)	"	"	A. W. Carmichael	"	166 E. 51st St., Savannah, Ga.
12	Ellison Ellwood C.(x)	"	"	Mrs. C. Ellison	Mother	181 Hoyt St. Fond Dulac, Wisc
13	Hanscom Austin F. (Y)	"	"	A. F. Hanscom	Father	Williams,Minn
14	Hardin John G. (X)	"	"	N. G. Hardin	"	602 Gr.Bldg Atlanta, Ga.
15	Hughes Shelby G. (X)	"	"	G.L.Hughes	"	Cor 19th and Bar- nard Ave. Nash- ville, Tenn.
16	Lefold Gray H. (X)	"	"	R. Lefold	"	6030 Tulip St Tacony,Phila,Pa.
17	Lowry Francis D. (Y)	"	"	W. B. Lowry	"	946 Corona St. Denver, Colo.
18	McCloskey Frank H. (X)	"	"	Mrs. H. McCloskey	Mother	Marietta, Pa.
19	Perrin Payson A. (X)	"	"	A.L.Perrin	Father	Wyman & Gorden Co. Bradley St. Worcester, Mass.
20	Raynsford James W. (X)	"	"	Willard C. Raynsford	"	97 Rhode IslandAv Detroit,Mich.
21	Robinson Jesse M. (X)	"	"	Mrs. W. L. Peet	Mother	3514 Newark St Washington,D.C.
22	Tickner Reginald W (X)	"	"	F.W.Tickner	Father	Valley Mold & Iron Co., Sharpsville, Pa.
23	VanCamp Roy K. (X)	"	"	Mrs. J. R. VanCamp	Mother	Punta Gorda,Fla

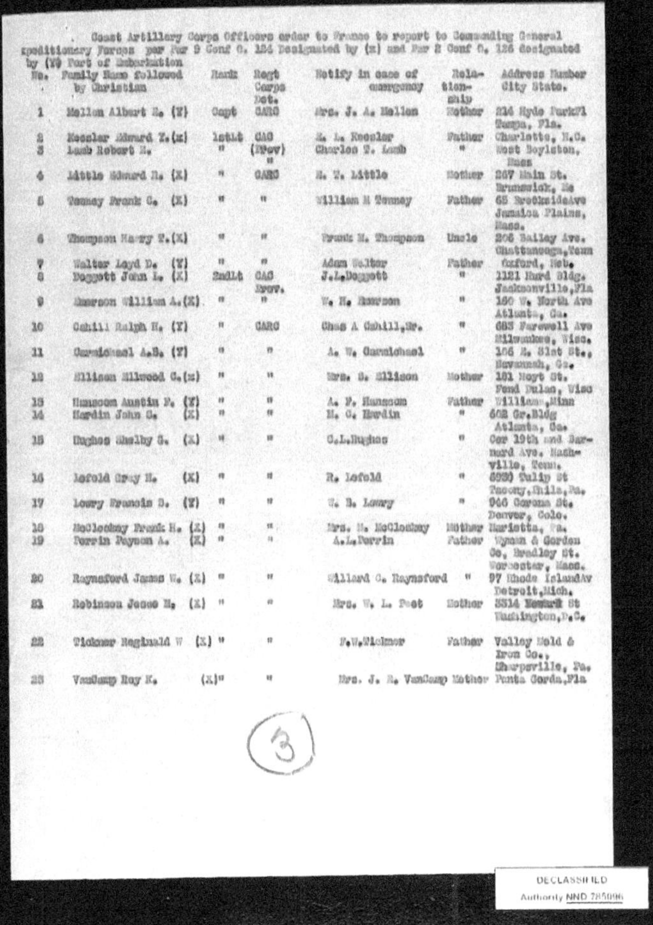

Military list of Americans sent to France

JOHN LOCKE DOGGETT JR

A note on the text

This is not a novel. It is not rife with metaphors and similes, it does not have gracefully flowing syntax and it certainly has not been reviewed by a team of professional editors. Not that there is anything wrong with that - *Catch-22* and *All Quiet on the Western Front* are both military and literary masterpieces. But this is not that.

This is a diary; a World War I, on the front lines, diary. Everything you read is exactly how it was written, including any broken sentences, misspelled French words, and outdated colloquialisms. There are some days his entries are rich with action and emotion, and other days he cannot muster more than a few words.

This diary is simultaneously disturbing and hopeful. It is both exciting and boring. It depicts the toils and tedium of the Front lines. It is raw, tangible and not trying to impress anybody. If you are looking for a romanticized story that glorifies combat, or a poignant critique of capitalist warfare - this book is not for you.

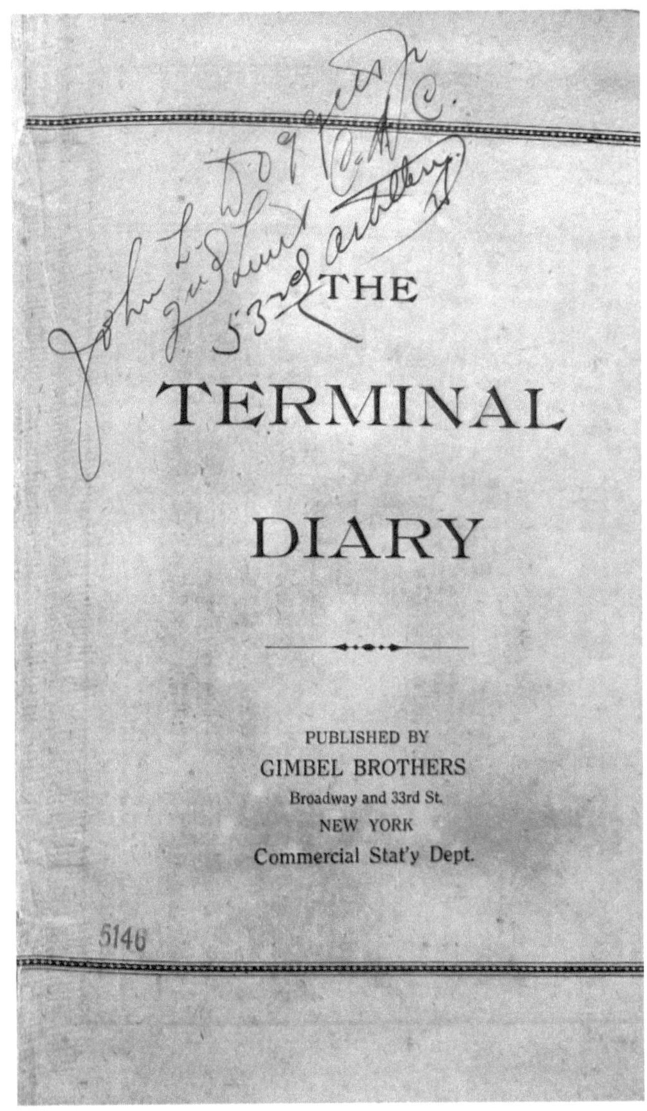

THE

TERMINAL

DIARY

PUBLISHED BY

GIMBEL BROTHERS

Broadway and 33rd St.

NEW YORK

Commercial Stat'y Dept.

5146

JOHN LOCKE DOGGETT JR

Introduction

John Locke Doggett Jr. was born January 14, 1893 in Jacksonville, Florida. He came from a wealthy, prominent family whose direct lineage in the United States traces back to 1637 and, by marriage, back to the Mayflower.

He studied pre-law at Yale and, upon graduating, obtained a law degree from Harvard University. Directly after this he enlisted as an officer in US Army.

Doggett was a member of the 53rd Artillery of the Army Coast Artillery Corps in the American Expeditionary Forces during the First World War from September 1917 until Armistice day. During his time at the Front, Doggett rose to the rank of Captain and, along with this 11-month daily record, took over 500 front-line photographs documenting the death, destruction and humanity of the Great War.

Part of the Second Battalion, Battery H and stationed in Haussimont, France, he fought in the Second Battle of Marne and the Battle of Chateau-Thierry in July 1918. The very last offensive of the German Army, these battles were an integral turning point in the war and marked the start of the unyielding Allied advance. In September of 1918 he fought in the

Battle of Saint-Mihiel, an offensive led by General John J. Pershing involving the AEF and 110,000 French troops. The attack was the first major offensive led primarily by the United States and established the stature of the US as a dominant and critical force in the war, which culminated in Armistice Day just 57 days later.

Doggett and his battery were in near-constant conflict with German bombardments. They saw action across France in Haussimont, Somme Suippe, Camp Nantivet, the Argonne Forrest, and many other regions throughout the Marne, Muese, and Aube. Doggett and his battery were awarded the Croix de Guerre with 1 Palm by the French Government for acts of heroism in combat.

Armed with naivety and a camera, Doggett learned that gas is "the worst modern way to torture humans", silence is more unnerving than battle, and nothing smells worse than dead horse.

When Doggett first entered the war, his privileged life seemed to follow him. He took regular weekend trips to Paris where he stayed in 5-star hotels, dined with Winston Churchill, was visited by vacationing relatives, and perused the Parisian Grand Boulevards. However, soon after, Fourth of July fire-works were replaced with 60,000 rounds of exploding ammunition, turndown service was performed by rodents, and luxury was now measured in number of baths per month.

Travel took him from blown out churches to concerts of the renowned Harlem Hellfighters and back to the trenches in time for gas drill instruction. Depictions of the gore and grandeur of war are accompanied by scenes of compassion for man's greatest predator – himself. Amidst nightly bombardments, the 53rd Artillery managed to care for stray pets while slowly descending into deeper apathy for their own kind. Throughout the diary, we see Doggett grow less concerned with letters from home and more concerned with staying in the action at the Front.

John Locke Doggett Jr

JOHN LOCKE DOGGETT JR

1

January

Tuesday January 1

Entered Fort Monroe[1] September 22nd, 1917

Received Commission in regular army October 26th following exams from civil life taken at Fort Screven[2] on July 23rd.

Volunteered for Foreign Service on November 25th – was accepted and given leave of absence until December 10th. Paid hurried visits to MBS and Louie – and reported at N.Y. on December 10th ready to embark. Delayed in N.Y. City for 17 days – finally sailing on SS Philadelphia, American Line on December 27th – was very sick at time of sailing with grippe[3]. While leaving harbor, US officers allowed to appear on deck. Answered roll call. Ship highly camouflaged in green, blue, and pink rectangles. Ship very fast and trip made without convoy up to submarine zone.

Assigned to stateroom 406 with 2nd lieutenants Davis W.S.R.F.A. from Columbus, Georgia, and D'Evelyn W.S.R.E. from California. Morning of 28th all passengers and officers (150) were assigned to lifeboats and attendance at daily drill was compulsory.

Our course secured to run North first as we entered Newfoundland. Banks in a dense fog. The sea was very smooth.

On the 28th I gave up the ghost[4] and remained in my bunk. I realized that my attack of grippe had developed into quinsy being aggravated by the cold, damp weather. Ship's doctor had attended me and stated he was afraid to operate on my throat because of danger of a slip while boat was in motion. I was removed to a room by myself. I slipped up to watch target practice of the gun crews and was gratified by the remarkable shots made. Throat became worse, and for the rest of trip (five days) I ate nothing, being unable to swallow anything solid. Soup made me seasick, so water was my only friend. While ice compressions relieved my throat somewhat. Sea very rough.

Was informed that two American destroyers had come up to convoy us. We were now in the danger zone – very rough weather, and as for me, I would have welcomed any sub!

1

Tuesday Jan 1

Entered Fort Monroe Sept 27th 1917. Received Commission in Regular Army Oct 26th following Exams from civil life taken at Fort Screven on July 3rd. Volunteered for Foreign service on Nov 25th - was accepted and given leave of absence until Dec 10th. Paid hurried visits to M.B.S. and home - and reported at N.Y. on Dec 10th ready to embark. Delayed in N.Y. City for 17 days - finally sailing on S.S. Phila- delphia, American Line on Dec 27th - was very sick at time of sailing with grippe -. While leaving harbor no officer allowed to appear on deck. Answered roll call. Ship highly camouflaged in green, blue and pink rectangles. Ship very fast and trip made without convoy up to Submarine zone. Assigned to Stateroom 406 with Lts Davis W.S.R.F.A. from Columbus Ga and D'Evelyn U.S.R.E. from California. Morning of 28th all passengers and officers (150) were as-

Page out of the original Terminal Diary - January 1
1918

Friday January 4

Abscess broke in my throat. Weather cleared. My spirits rose to a high pitch. I bathed in a huge tub of salt water. Shaved for the first time since I'd left New York. Ate a whale of a breakfast and went on deck. We were now in Iris sea. Very smooth but weather intensely cold. The destroyers remained close friends, circling us while we maintained a zigzag course. It seemed impossible that death-dealing "subs" should be hovering under such clear skies in deep-blue waters. An English "squid", a long dirigible, joined the convoy and sailed around, looking for the shadows of subs. The guns crews on the Phill[5] were on constant watch.

Everyone seemed to be on such a strain that it made me right sleepy. I went below as I was tired of dragging the damn life preserver around.

We arrived at the mouth of the Mersey River, Liverpool, late Friday night (4th). We entered the harbor and awoke next morning expecting to land and see the town – no such luck. We spent the day aboard the ship, watching the queer customs of the inhabitants of Liverpool. It seems that one must never sit on a ferry boat but it is customary to walk around madly always to the right like rats – *n'est-ce pas?*

Opposite us lay the Leviathan – the huge German liner

Fatherland which the US had seized. She was stuck in the mud! Too big for the harbor. She carried 12,000 troops on the initial trip.

We docked at 7:00 pm but we [were] not allowed to land until 9:00 when we were marched to the railroad station and I saw an English train for the first time. That's all we saw; Liverpool was pitch dark. It seemed strange to be an American soldier on English soil! We rode from 9:30 pm until 5:00 am in the Lilliputian[6] coaches. No beds, but fairly comfortable.

Sunday January 6

Arrived Winchester at 5:00 am and walked two miles to an American "rest camp" – a very fine camp – cement houses. I roomed with Carl Mills, a second Lieutenant in J.W. – we had iron beds – seven blankets a piece – a stove – plenty of soft coal and a willing orderly. My hunger defeated a desire to sleep and I got up after an hours' sleep and welcomed corned beef!

Carl slept like a big Swede, so McFadden and I determined to go to town. He hooked a ride in and [we] retired [in the] Royal Hotel where we received our first English reception – very cordial, and I liked the English from now on. The Royal gave me a hot tub – a hot meal but not much of it and no coal. England is on war rations of food and fuel.

Wrote letters to Mom and Reddie, but too cold for any intensive thought.

We returned to camp after squaring our bill and spent the afternoon and night doping out – bobs[7], two pennies, farthings, and pounds. No orders for us at camp.

Monday January 7th

Fortified with a knowledge of the value of English money, we put in our pay vouchers and McFadden and I hooked another ride to town – this time in a Ford taxi driven by a girl. I survived the ride. McFadden and I purchased our Sam Brown's and proceeded to "do" Winchester and also search for a regular meal – for this latter the "God-be-got" him at lunch proved to be a failure.

McFadden and I visited "The Castle" of King Arthur's fame and American Indians. Winchester is the oldest city in England and was the capital for centuries – very interesting, but our stomachs were lean and the search for food was resumed. I spied some pheasants in a fish-market. Broiled pheasants was a pleasant thought. We met Mr. Till, the little confectioner. The bargain is made and Tuesday was the date.

At night, McFadden, Roby (Robinson) and I attended a pantomime: "Dick Whittington" – Horatio Alger stuff set to music[8]. No men – all girls in trousers. The English townie keeps his hat on in the theater – and spits accurately through his smoke rings.

Tuesday January 8th

We had our party with Mr. Till, McFadden, McClosky, Robinson, Mills, and myself. McFadden and I bought three huge pheasants. Mr. Till prepared them together with his own fresh vegetables and a marvelous chocolate pudding. A rare feast served in a room to ourselves, big warm fire and Mr. Till, master mason, as chief entertainer – "Josie" a modern philosopher and an English gentleman.

We received orders to report ready to leave the rest camp at 8:00 am, Wednesday. Regretted to leave Winchester – but we hoped to get to London as we received our paychecks and there were new fields to explore – there is a certain thrill in being ordered to report ready to "leave" – as we never know where we are headed – I guess it is all part of the delightful indefiniteness of army life.

An American repository overseas, carrying various canons and mortars

Wednesday January 9th

The orderly lost his drag with me when he called us at 5:00 am – took out our baggage and reported mess at 6:00 am – however, I had learned that it's just folly to ignore a mess call, and I arose to pay court to a plate of corned beef (I'd call it "bull!") and army coffee (it's delightfully indefinite, too).

We reported at headquarters and were told to catch the 9:40 train, which we discovered went to Southampton. We filled a train of first-class coaches and rode in luxury – followed by the Montana National Guard.

We arrived at Pier No. 2, Southampton – were dismissed until 5:00 pm. I bought some cigarettes from the Montana boys who had not been paid for two months and McFadden and I as usual searched for a meal – we fed up at Shorts, and returned an hour later for more (we could only buy one meal at a time – no seconds). We visited the old Morman church, etc and returned to Pier No. 2 – we were assigned to a captured German cattleship "The Huntscraft" for our trip across the channel.

Thursday January 10th

150 casual officers and 500 of the Montana troops – everything pitch dark on deck, very cold – the hold was truly a house for cattle – lime and whitewash on the stalls – general filth on the floor – no place to sleep. I made my bed on a water bucket and was lucky.

Just before sailing, one Montana boy's soul revolted and he was carried away – I determined not to kick my bucket. Very rough night – British destroyers on all sides. The English channel lived up to it's "rep" and became so tempestuous that a large water vat (for cattle) broke loose and sprayed everyone in the hold – the lime reacted and Roby and I crawled into the boiler room at 4:00 am. I slept on an iron railing over the engines twenty feet below – the possibility of a long fall meant nothing to me. I swore at the grease instead.

Woke up to find ourselves off the city of Harvé – we were anchored in the beloved English channel and had to wait till 8:00 that night for a place on deck – throughout the day I was a prey to the exorbitant prices demanded by the Chinese crew, who I bribed for food – and also more cold and no place to sit. I'm off the Channel for life.

Friday January 11th

Docked at Harvé, and all the romance of "setting foot on French soil" was knocked out of me when I slipped in the mud – then waded through two miles of it to rest camp No. 2. "Rest" here is a misnomer. We were rationed 5 blankets and a straw mattress to cover bunks with iron slabs for springs. Roby and I bunked together. McFadden and Mills, having been sent to camp No. 1, we did not see them anymore. Roby located a mess room and we did our bit on hot dogs, a loaf of bread, and hot tea at midnight. After that Channel trip, the iron slab felt like velvet springs and I slept like a tired second Lieutenant should, and I missed breakfast!

I found hot chocolate and sweet cakes at the YMCA hut – this is a great organization! No permits were granted to leave camp so Harvé remains unseen. Our chief diversion here was to get acquainted with French weather. There was not much variety – if it's not raining – it's damp. The sun never shines in France during the winter. Maybe it's apropos of the war.

The officers' mess at this camp was excellent – only I've a suspicion that the Journey Sergeants who run it take advantage of our ignorance of the value of a Sow, Centimes, and Francs.

Saturday January 12th

All C.A.C. officers ordered to leave at 4:00 pm. Such pleasant instructions are not received often. Rest camp No. 2 was left without regrets. We found our baggage floating in the mud and rescued it. Then made our way to the station and stole a glimpse of Harvé. John Bull has recruited large numbers of Zulu laborers – it seemed almost like home to see a real black man once more – they're a real happy lot. We passed many German prisoners who scowled as a Boche should.

At the station Roby and I got lost from the crowd because we were lured to a news dropper's stand by "La Vie Paris Illumé" Mon Dieu – quelle Francais! We almost went to Paris by mistake but finally rejoined our flock in the freight yards – we seized a first-class compartment and took Beddleson on with us. Roby and I and Biddly spread ourselves and kept out all comers. Our orders read to Mailly Heavy Artillery school. No Paris with wine, women, and song. We lived on carved salmon and hardtack for twenty-four hours.

Sunday January 13th

The route to Mailly led us around Paris through Troyes[9] and up to the battlefield of the Marne[10]. I confess I had a queer feeling while being driven through the streets of Mailly, Aube[11], – of shelled houses nothing remained but lovely walls. To make matters worse, it was moonlit specters? Ghosts? No. Simply war, and I almost forgot to go to mass.

About 11:00 I was assigned to a hut – Roby drawing the bunk nearest me. Our baggage arrived and I, having neglected to buy a cot, crawled on the floor in my bedding roll. After things had quieted down, I asked the orderly what the steady rumble and deep roar was – "Oh, them's the big boys talking on the front – thirty miles off". Sleeping on the battlefield of the Marne – thirty miles from the frontline trenches! I felt like a white rabbit with pink eyes – but I had lots of company.

Monday January 14th

We discovered that only 150 of the 500 C.A.C. officers had arrived and that we were free to do as we pleased until the rest of the bunch came in – so Roby and I spent the next week sightseeing – sort of a grim way to seek pleasure but already we were used to the numbers from the front – we knew the bite couldn't reach us so the bark lost its power. Mailly is one of the large rest camps of the French. Here we found infantry, artillery – light and heavy, anti-aircraft, and aviation. There are about [*number crossed out*] American troops present already. The heavy artillery school is in the center of the French section of the camp – or rather the Senegalese section.

Sunday Jan 13

Salmon and hard tack for twenty four hours. The route to Mailly led us around Paris, through Troyes and up to the battlefields of the Marne. I confess I had a queer feeling while being driven thru the streets of Mailly, Aube,— shelled houses nothing remained but lonely walls - to make matters worse it was moonlight. Spectres? ghosts? No - simply war and I almost forgot to go to mess. About three o'clock I was assigned to a hut - Roby drawing the bunk nearest me. Our baggage arrived and I having neglected to buy a cot crawled on the floor in my bedding roll. After things had quieted down, I asked the orderly what the steady rumble and deep roar was - "Oh - thems the big boys Talking on the front - thirty miles off." Sleeping on the battlefield of the Marne - 30 miles from the front line trenches! I felt like a white rabbit with pink eyes — but I had lots of company!

Page out of the original Terminal Diary - January 13, 1918

A WWI era mechanical trench digger

Tuesday January 15th

We were called over to school and were allowed to state our preferences as to what branches of the C.A.C. we wished to specialize in. There were five in all and my choice ran in order thus: 1. Heavy artillery school; 2. Tractor school; 3. Anti-aircraft; 4. Trench Mortars; 5. Aerial Observers. I failed to get assigned to the school and as yet do not know what duty we will be given.

The Trench Mortar boys are known as the suiciders – in the trenches they fire small guns with black powder and invariably draw the Boche artillery fire and zip! – it is a great life while it lasts.

The aerial observers average 21 hours in the air before a Bosch pots him – so what's the use. Oh, this is a fine war!

I have run into Bill Badham from Birmingham, also Charlie Jones – and three men from Florida – Captain Mullon (Bradentown), recruits Van Camp (Bartow), Collins (Tampa), and Morrain of Fleming and Fleming Jacksonville. Also met a cousin of Marie Lassiters but enough of this, let's get back to the war.

"The Trench Mortar boys are known as the suiciders
[...] it is a great life while it lasts." January 15, 1918

Wednesday January 16th

I gave a party at Jeanne D'Arc and I am here thinking this was my birthday – I find I'm a day late! Roby and I took a walk to "the tanks". We slipped past the French sentry due to a successful camouflage of mud acquired on the six-mile hike and soon found ourselves surrounded by glimmering *poilus*[12] and Tanks by the hundred. – Big fat oblong movers moving with great alacrity across practice trenches and spreading demolition in the rows of imaginary Boches.

We were enjoying ourselves hugely and parading my "*Parlez*" until a French Lieutenant came up – the *poilu* vanished and I forgot my French – "*Defendu d'eutter, m'sieur!*" – "No speak French, *Mon Souer.*" – "*Poo-poo*" – "*Pah-pah*" – "Whoah – back up" – *et mon ami Francais est vaiucu*! It's funny how dumb an American can be, and when that French Lieutenant told me I had done wrong to enter camp without a permit and that I must leave immediately – oh goodness Miss Agnes – How dumb I was!!

Thursday January 17th

We next visited the anti-aircraft camp – situated on a high hill. Here we found no permits necessary and I dressed my *parlez* up in Sunday style – ran an "open shop" for my cars and waded in. Anti-aircraft is very technical but this gun had only been used twice in the last year – I think this sounds like an attractive branch of the service – had I but known! The *poilus* here ran their own wine cellar – I think they had an onion garden *aussi*, from the pungent odors in their dugouts. I braved our inspection of their quarters and let it be said – the Senegalese have nothing on this crew, while a Billy goat is put to shame!

Friday January 18th

In Mailly is a fine example of German marksmanship and barbarianism. A shelled church. A gaping hole in the roof inside a mass of crumbled shelled walls; demolished pews, the alter fire-racked – the whole little church a mass of ruins. Roby and I stood gazing over this from a broken window. Then we saw something I shall remember a long time – a French corporal entered the church – made his way through the ruins, and pausing here and there, seemed to be looking for something – we watched him in silence. He marched to the alter and stopped before a figure in the shadow of a cracked wall. Fell on his knees and prayed. This gay blue uniform prostrate before a dim statue seemed incongruous in such oppressive surroundings – but such is France. His prayer finished. The soldier arose, and kept looking at the statue. Moved by intense curiosity, Roby and I entered the church, and as we neared the figure, we were astonished to see that amidst all this devastation the figure stood intact – unharmed – it was the likeness of a woman. The *poilu* turned and whispered "How could it be otherwise – that is our Jeanne D'Arc".

"A shelled church. A gaping hole in the roof inside a mass of crumbled shelled walls; demolished pews, the alter fire-racked" January 18, 1918

A shelled church in Mailly, France: ""How could it be otherwise – that is our Jeanne D'Arc" - January 18, 1918

Saturday January 19th

Another instance of German methods and French blindness to anything else but victory was impressed upon this Saturday. Bill Badham, Charlie Jones and I started cross-country which we found less muddy than the roads. We had no objective – but our course led us to the center of the battlefield of the Marne – around Sommes-Sous. The fields here are dotted with the graves of French buried where they fell – each is decorated with the Tricolors, a wooden cross with a name cut into it and underneath this appears the single word *"soldat"*[13]. Before one of these graves we stopped. It was off on a hill by itself and attracted our attention because it seemed well kept yet solitary. As we stood near it a boy about 12 came whistling down the hill – and I tried my *parlez*. The grave was his fathers who had been shot down by a German aviator while he was plowing – a noncombatant! The lad had lost 2 brothers in Belgium – his mother was out nursing wounded *poilus* and he – yes – he was going to fight too – for this is France and he was a Frenchman. We left him praying at the grave. A few moments later we heard him whistling on the other side of the hill.

Sunday January 20th

Today Roby and I bought *un poulet* – had it roasted at *Jeanne D'arcs* and fed up on fried potatoes, jam, war bread, and some precious real butter. Walked to anti-aircraft station. Soft job. The darned thing has only been fired twice in a year!

Monday January 21st

I find I am hopelessly far behind so in order to catch up and make a real diary of this instead of an auto-biography I shall simply notate events up to the present time and fill in later as opportunity presents itself.

Walked to the carrier pigeon station. Here pigeons are transported to the front and sent "over the top" in case of dire need and distress when in no man's land. The *poilus* release them and soon the carriers have home a message to headquarters.

"The fields here are dotted with the graves of French buried where
they fell - each is decorated with the tricolors, a wooden cross with a
name cut into it and underneath this appears the single word 'soldat' "
– January 19, 1918

Tuesday January 22nd

I discovered definitively that I would not be assigned to the heavy artillery school. Up railroad mounts for mine.

Wednesday January 23rd

Heavy Artillery School opens. Roby and I are separated. We meet Lieutenant La Marque and are invited to dinner with the 1st Battalion of French infantry, (dismounted cavalry) just returned from nine months in the trenches. We sing Le Marseille and hum the Star-Spangled Banner but promise to learn the words.

Thursday January 24th

General rejoicing over arrival of laundry – 63 pieces!

Friday January 25th

Formal French mess – I sit on Major's right – and *parlez* my finest. The prince is on my right and La Marque opposite Bill Badham and Charlie Jones at Major's left (and Bill in front). We were the first officers of U.S.A. these French had seen and *pardonnez* but we really did bring home the bacon.

Promised to go horseback riding with La Marque Sunday on a French cavalry horse.

Saturday January 26th

Returned from a long walk to find I had been ordered to leave Mailly at 6:00 Sunday. I found I had been assigned to the French Artillery Tractor School at Camp de St. Maur near Fontenoy sur Bois. This meant absolutely nothing to me – I didn't even know what part a tractor played in this war. Had to pack up and leave a call with the orderly for 4:30 am.

Sunday January 27th

Charlie Jones was assigned to the tractor school also. We spent twelve long hours going 60 miles. The trains ran so slowly that it was possible to dismount in a village, go in, buy a cheese, hunk o' war bread, and light wine and catch up with our coach again! We got dope that Fontenoy sur Bois was fifteen minutes from Paris! Oh boy!

Arrived Fontenoy at light – no one to meet us – waited at station for two hours and finally received an order giving us Paris permission for two and a half days! Paris – hotel Continental – a huge room – lace curtains – two beds – and a genuine hot tub. Charlie and I bunked together.

Monday January 28th

Breakfast in bed of hot chocolate, bread, butter and jam — the universal French *dejeuner*. Today, Tuesday, and Wednesday, we saw Paris – in all its glory. Phoned Mrs. E.W. Roberts – Aunt Claire, and she acted as pilot – while I spent the three hundred Francs I had borrowed from Roby.

Saw the airplane of the famous Captain Gunnery
Des Invalides
Notre Dame
Champs Elysees
Arc d'Triomphe
Basalisque de la Sacre Coeur
Louvre
Luxumbourg
Palais Royale
Palais des Beaux Arts

Caisse d'Epargne, a French bank in Paris that dealt
with currency exchange.

Tuesday January 29th

A glorious day on the grand boulevard.

Wednesday January 30th

At 2:00 pm we reported to Major Carson at Camp de St. Maur. We found out what the school was.

We were to handle the new 155 G.P.F. 16 inch mobile gun. It moves on tractors so we are here to study the theory and construction of the automobile under the best that France has. Can you make an automobile expert out of an embryonic lawyer?

The Major announced that we would work here for one month of the most intensive study. Then, we go either to the front or act as instructors at a second camp. But for each weekend we will be given 24-hour leave in Paris. What luck! For an American officer to enter Paris, a special permit is necessary – this is to hold down the deficiency of our expeditionary forces. Very few US soldiers or officers can be seen in Paris – we will be envied by all the men at Mailly.

Thursday January 31st

This morning at 12:30 am we were all awakened by a terrific booming and roar of high powered mortars. The Boches!

– the moon was brilliant, the stars out by the thousands. Every now and then there would be a lurid red flash – another roar and we know a bomb dropped by one of the air-raiders had spread destruction and death in Paris. The French sent up flaming torches but the Boches were flying high – anti-aircraft guns were useless but we could hear the crack of machine guns of the French and Hun planes. Finally there was stillness in Paris – fire – death – devastation – German tactics.

"Every now and then there would be a lurid red flash – another road and we know a bomb dropped by one of the air-raiders has spread destruction and death in Paris." – January 31st 1918

A soldier lies dead and badly burnt.

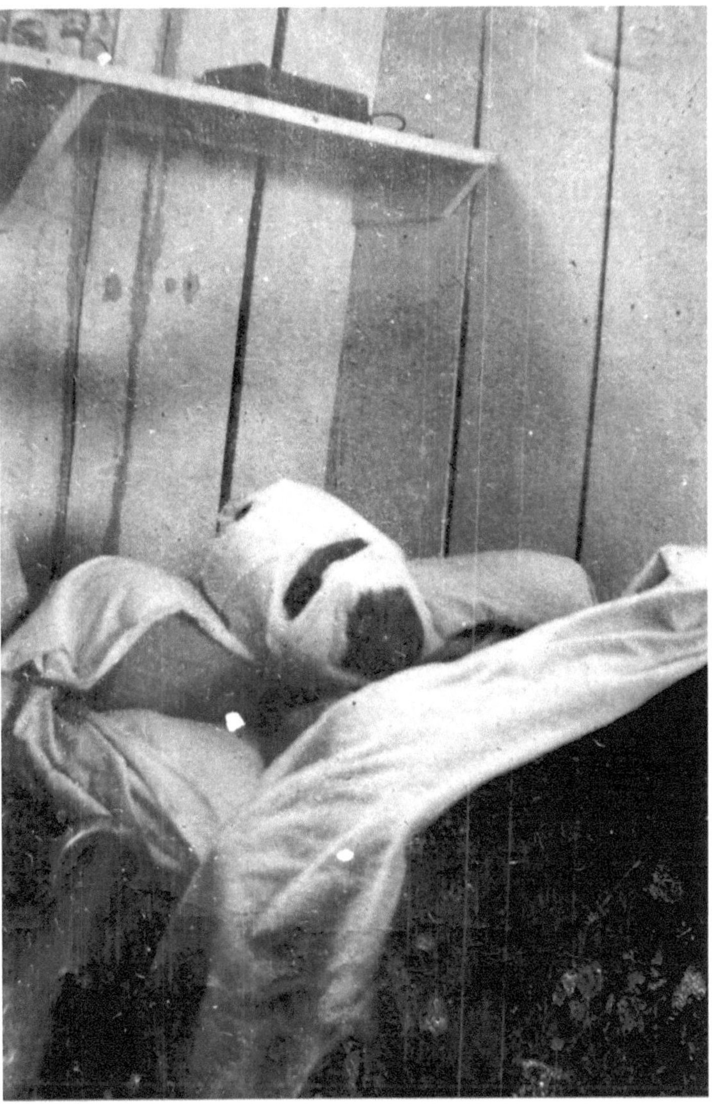

A soldiers lies wounded and covered in bandages
while recovering at a Red Cross dressing station.

2

February

Friday February 1st

Today we inspected the results of the air raid – within a quarter of an hours' walk from us a block of houses was destroyed and its people killed. Paris lost about 150 but no large buildings. One out of 40 attacking Gotha bombers was brought down. The Huns won but we learned that the French were preparing a return raid on Maunsheux.

Saturday February 2nd

Paris again. Ran into Bill Barnett – he is stranded in Paris and is trying to get into the war US 1st, French second and British service third.

Saw Gaby Desbys and Harry Pilcur in Broadway girl

show which makes the costuming in the Winter Garden look
fur lined!

Sunday February 3rd

Dick Wilson slapped me on the back – of all persons to see
over here. Also met up with Carl Mills, McFadden and Wur-
ford – also Dutch Arnold from Yale. Phoned Aunt Claire
but she was busy – Cabled Momsey and Little Lady.

Monday February 4th

School again. Studied cylinders of motors.

Tuesday February 5th

Encore school. Studied timing system of auto.

Wednesday February 6th

Drove a big Panhard truck – 6 speeds forward! Stud-
ied pumping and circulation systems in motors. Introduced
Miss Baulord of Am Ex. Co. to the men in the school. She's
English but she has a French accent. Thinks it's violet.

Thursday February 7th

Paris – and French Generals visited the camp. The *poilus* men inspected and we had to go without a fire. Lots of mechanical maneuvers and bed is welcome. If I don't find some exciting dope to put down here soon I'm going to quit the job. This is not due to lack of imagination but blame it on a voluntary self-sworn determination to record only truths herein. So I may put on my specs when I'm a Grandpa and tell the kids just how twas without working to make a good story of it!

But I couldn't stir up a Red Cross contribution out of this so far.

Friday February 8th

The chief value of Friday is that it is the day before Saturday. Hence we can "Thang On" until *demain* and sleep with dreams of Paris.

Today was a bore – two lectures – neither interesting, and an extra dose of mechanical maneuvers.

Major Carson announced that 10 men from the school would be selected for special work. Those will be the 10 highest standard. The rest of us will be made instructors – I never thought I'd become a pedagogue when I signed up against the Huns. We have two cases of mumps in camp!

Saturday February 9th

Walked to Jincumes with Chas. There we found a "sub" for Paris. Met Bill Barnett at Adam's Express Company and dined at Duval's. I had two steaks, a ham omelet, French fried confiture, *et des apricots*! Every thing was rosy until two *jolie femmes* sat beside us and looked like "give us a glass of wine"! The only trouble with Paris is that there are too many women. Never before have I been chased out of a café by a pretty girl – generally it is vise versa! Charlie and I returned to camp at 10 and had to walk 3 miles because no tramway was run in Jincumes after 9:30—these French fear the Gothas like an American does a coutey – or cutey!

Sunday February 10th

Charlie finally woke up and we hiked for Paris – lunched with Aunt Claire and Mr. Roberts. Bill, Chas and I hired a taxi and chased around Paris viewing the effects of the Boche air raid. Back to camp and work. Today I cabled Little Lady and the family. Gee – I sure wish I had a bunch of long letters from home!

Mail being delivered to the troops

Monday February 11th

There`s something discouraging about Mondays – I always

wish it was Sunday again and yet I am a firm believer in the "it's a great life if you don't weaken" strep and I do feel weaken after laying around useless on weekends. Today we tackled artillery again – also carburetors and the theory of the ignition system. This dope is getting deep, I'm afraid I'm running another bluff. The American mail cam in today – I drew a bill from Langrock! Oh – Jam - i - lee where fore art thou?

Tuesday February 12th

We had a false alarm on the air raid last night and the *poilus* wasted plenty of steam on their sirens – but neither this nor the fact that today is Lincoln's birthday disturbed my tin house sleep. I am truly so fat that I am ashamed to send home some pictures of me laughing [face drawn in text]. The head is not necessary to portray for the purpose of this illustration.

Today I was examined to qualify as an expert driver of autos! Some cinch – only I wish I'd had an enemy in the car with me! We are being inspected by a genuine Colonel – I shall take pills tonight!

Wednesday February 13th

Bill Barbett came out for dinner and we had a glorious bull session – we gave our enemies –– and praised our friends –

Poor old Bill is S.O.L. – he is trying to get into the French artillery as Uncle Sam has turned him down physically.

Thursday February 14th

I've been chauffeuring a big Renault tractor all afternoon through heavy mud – 'twas quite some fun but yea boa – I'm no Sampson, and I had my troubles Jack Johnsoning that steering wheel.

Friday February 15th

More mechanical maneuvering – this time we dragged our gun through a French forest, i.e., not more than ten trees are ever allowed in one French forest – ours had four!

This afternoon we attended an excellent lecture on the gears, differential and rear axle. *Je suis fatigue – Bonsoir!*

Saturday February 16th

Paris encore: big feed – big show – big tub – big water – big bed – big sleep – *Finis.*

Sunday February 17th

Encore Paris!
Breakfast awed.
Shampoo – haircut – more tubs.
Phoned Aunt Claire but she was sick hence no dance.
Back to camp and study.

Monday February 18th

A false alarm from the alert started every anti-aircraft gun in Paris and we crawled out of our bunks to view the shrapnel display, only to be ordered indoors. The new regulations are: windows covered, lights out at ten, remain inside during a raid and sleep on first floors of hotels in Paris.

Tuesday February 19th

Routine!

Routine drill instruction

Wednesday February 20th

Field maneuvers about ten miles from here which lasted

the entire day. I shall always remember the filthy street urchins in the little village – easily 80% were crippled.

The French served a splendid lunch to us in the Field – almost reminded me of Momsey's wonderful picnics –but that's a might little almost.

Thursday February 21st

Mail from Home. Three huge envelopes full of mail from Momsey – my first real letters. I've read until I'm dizzy but oh – how good it is to hear from those we love and – Momsey, Momsey how I love you – I know you would find some way to hurry me some news and I've been so darned lonely – now – I'm as happy as a kid after his first news of Santa Claus.

Friday February 22nd

Routine – Washington's Birthday, *Ah oui*.

Saturday February 23rd

Paris.

Sunday February 24th

Lunch again with Aunt Claire –she surely is a peach.

Monday February 25th

Let it be said that he who drives a big tractor for 12 hours throughout the night is an object of admiration – therefore I admire myself as I was given this honor during our night maneuvers – Oh *mes pauvres jambes*.

Tuesday, February 26th

Slept one hour – this makes my total for the last 36 straight. We drove out today to Barou – (Bo Bo!) Castle. The grounds were beautiful – a real castle but all the romance was lost when we were shown the place we must place our guns – on top of a mountain in a fort defending Paris! It hardly seems possible that our huge tractors and guns can make the climb... but watch us!

Wednesday, February 27th

The day has been devoted to a stud of the Ford Motor Car. I have the respect for the abilities of the tin lizzie and also for the ingenuity of its constructor.

Thursday, February 28th

We woke at 5:30. Wet – cold – pitch dark. Poor breakfast etc. My job as usual was to handle the tractor. I drove 15 minutes to the Barous estate and arrived with my gun half hour ahead of schedule. We puddled up the mountain – placed our gun in position and as a reward we are served lunch in the Barous Barn!

The French Minister of Artillery, two French Generals, scores of Majors were present to watch the Sammies get stuck – we beat the French ward! I was never so tired.

JOHN LOCKE DOGGETT JR

3

March

Friday March 1st

The colonel slung a bunch of bull this morning at our furnace, but the dope is this: School is over and I'm one of the grads in automobiles wow! I wonder what a cylinder is!

The question is: what's to become of me? I'm a lawyer mechanist! It looks as if I would get to the front but I must first serve in turn as an instructor. I have a splendid sense of humor in regards to my knowledge of autos, so I expect to have a mar – ve –lous time!

Saturday March 2nd

Permit to Paris for the supposedly last time.

Ran into Clarence Mendel at the university union. We bummed around town and ate at Premiers – splendid clams, scallops, steak and French fries.

Hooked a hot bath at Blunney's room and hit my own feathers at 9:45!

Sunday March 3rd

Slept late – cause I like to lie abed on Sunday mornings. Paris is a sea of mushy snow.

Received my first letters from Reddie – I'm just the luckiest man in this world.

Back to camp, and sent a bunch of letters home.

Friday Mar 1

The Col. slung a bunch of Bull this morning at Conference but the dope is this — School is over and I'm one of the grads in Automobiles now! I wonder what a cylinder is! The question is — what's to become of me? I'm a lawyer mechanist! It looks as if I would get to the Front but I must first serve my turn as an instructor. I have a splendid sense of humor in regards to my knowledge of autos so I expect to have a mar - vel - ious time!

Photo from the original Terminal Diary - March 1, 1918

Monday March 4th

The *finis* of the Tractor School, and had to face a mess bill of 285 francs. "We" gave French instructors a banquet and then hiked to Paris – got a good hot tub, plus a glorious bed.

Ordered to Mailly.

Tuesday March 5th

Breakfast at Duvals – and off to the jail *a l'Est*.

Discovered the loss of my suitcase ! ! ! ! Irish grief!

Spent four hours in Châlus – (which the Boche has since bombed) also saw the famous Miss Antebell from NY in the GMCA but she sold tickets which accounts for my *beaucoup* eating!

Arrived Mailly about 7:30 pm. Assigned to building U-22 of Measles "pest".

Battery H marches through a destroyed town in Châlus

Wednesday March 6th

Reported 9:00 am. Am waiting for orders.

Thursday March 7th

I live between O-22 and Jeanne D'arc.

Friday March 8th

Much mail from home – Hence *plus d'lettres chez moi.*

Saturday March 9th

Orders received –

Am assigned to 53rd Artillery C.A.C. And report immediately at Haussimont – 10 km from here. What an existence to lead.

Reported – was assigned to Battery "H" – as green as any recruit ever was and I am an officer!

Sunday March 10th

I laid in bed trying to get acclimated! Also practicing commands on my orderly[14] – "Woody" – fits his brains.

Monday March 11th

I begin military life in earnest:
6:00 *Reveille*
6:15 Assemble
6:20 Recall
7-8 Breakfast

8:00 Formation – Infantry

9:15-11:30 Gun Drill

11:45 Officer's Call

12:00-1:00 Lunch

1:00 Formation; Classes for Enlisted Men

3:30 Battalion classes for officers

4:35 Call for Retreat

4:45 Retreat

Tuesday March 12th

I took command of Battery and stood my first Retreat. I got away with it but I can't walk on water yet!

Wednesday March 13th

I took my first shot at Infantry drill – i.e., I yelled loudly and watched what happened.

I joined Battalion class but what does a Tractor Man know about railway mounts?

Inspection of men and quarters.

Soldiers, some in gas masks, joke around by arranging their rifles into standing tipis.

Thursday March 14th

Drilled on guns – ours are the "19th" railway mounts.

We received orders to break camp. The 2nd Battalion is to entrain Sunday. The dope is construction work near Troyes.

Friday March 15th

Air raid alert – never touched us, but Châlus got it in the neck. I can hear the guns at the front infantry every night.

My quarters here are not the finest – tar papered walls smell and there are cracks innumerable which let in *beaucoup* cold air and it is cold! Nothing but candles for lights and my suitcase still lost – this is a great war.

Stood retreat.

A French 370mm railroad howitzer

Saturday March 16th

Final inspection of outfit and battery.

Sunday March 17th

We entrained at Sommes Sous at 6:30 pm. Rode all night. Cold prevented sleep.

Monday March 18th

We arrived Brunne-Le-Chateau Aube.

Detrained – Battery billeted in a huge barn.

My billet is with Madame Bonché – a splendid woman – a bed fit for Napoleon – plenty of air – table, chairs, fireplace, etc all in Cherry or something like that. Candles still!

Madame inspects me and I think has decided to like me – also Jeanne, her 10-year old granddaughter. Madame has lost 2 sons in the war – a 3rd is at the front and a 4th, Julian, is 17. He enters next year. MISTER Bonché is a traveling dry-goods merchant. He voyages from town to [town] in his "Grand Wagon".

I received news of my suitcase – tis found and en route. Allah is *tres bon*!

Madame's house forms two sides of a square courtyard, the barn and high-wall the other sides. In this courtyard about 20x20 the chicks and rabbits reign. The true French fashion: the cabinet and well are buddies – one 'longside the other. The family can't savvy why I neither smoke nor like to drink their "*vin ordinaire*". Perhaps they have a reason for not drinking their water.

I take check formation on the men at 7:00 am every morning, censor mail, attend Battalion classes, stand duty at battery office until 4 in the afternoons. Take my turn on the duty roster for service on the construction work. We are building ammunition dumps. Later we shall start classes for the battery "*non cours*" like algebra, artillery, etc.

Thursday March 21st

We are finally "oriented" – routine has started the Col. (Greig) paid us a visit today and Madame ate a chicken who died of appendicitis. She called it an "accident" and Madame and family ate head, feet, and even used the poor sick chick's blood for gravy! If that's economy, me for the fast reckless life!

Bath night – by Whistler Jr!

Friday March 22nd

Out with the men on the construction work

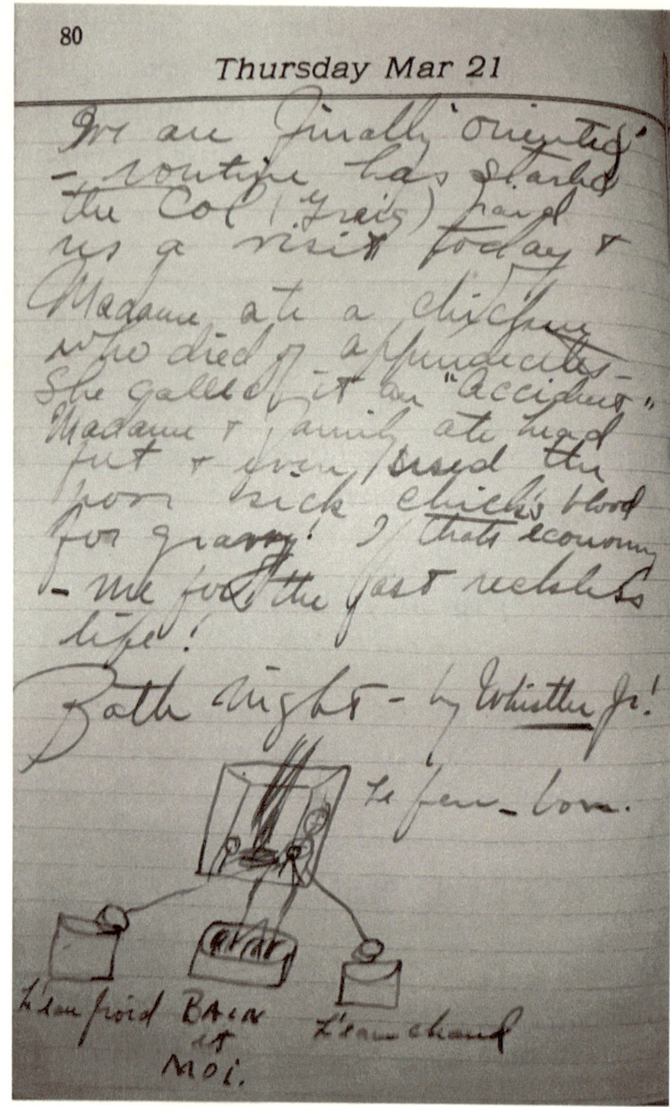

Photo from the original Terminal Diary - March 21, 1918

Saturday March 23rd

Slipped around the Chateau grounds. Here old man "Nat" used to play around. Beautiful place and well kept up.

Sunday March 24th

No church today and I slept around the clock! Rode thirty kilometers through the country on a hired bicycle. Great sport. Evans and I got tangled up in the ground fort. Many Boche prisoners – the mystic temple – we go home.

We are afraid of our own today. The whole village is now drunk.

Monday March 25th

My battery resembles a true picture of the "morning after" – there are two "A.W.O.L". A soldier is no good unless he is broken.

Lots of mail from home but none from Reddie[15] – it's a hard life.

Tuesday March 26th

Woody threatens to bayonet Julius because this youthful Frenchie is systematically swiping my shoe polish and saddle soap. Thank Heavens he can't wear my clothes.

The Madame likes my candles enough to "borrow one" now and then and the M'sier is using my paper for his personal correspondence. I am hugely flattered at the family's appreciation of my good taste but I am damned if I like this patronage – "steps have been taken to meet this attack."

Wednesday March 27th

Put on construction work again – looks as if we are here for two months.

The Boche has started his immense drive on the British Front – and Paris has been shelled by Cannon – "2' 40's" from a distance of over 100 kilometers – 62 miles! The world is on its toes and France is frenzied.

Thursday March 28th

The Boche has gone maybe 25 kilometers through the British and French – we hope this is British strategy – our 2,000,000 men are engaged in this terrific struggle. We can hear the artillery here easily.

Friday March 29th

Reported myself to the medico for treatment, looks as if I am in for more Frontal sinus – but the old suitcase came rolling in today and I don't care what happens.

Saturday March 30th

Capt. Lougino soaked us with a problem which will take easily three days to work – hence there's no dope for the diary tonight. Was out on the construction work today – it's raining like silly, cold and I've got frontal sinus – it's always a great life if you don't weaken and I'm going strong!

Two packages from Momsey and 15 letters in tonight's mail.

Sunday March 31ˢᵗ

Easer Sunday! Four thousand miles from home and not a ship in sight – rain and cold – mud – war – France – Hell boys, let's go home!

Muster ceremony held today – I've come to the conclusion that the best thing a lieutenant does for the Army is to draw pay and look wise – I'm only good at the latter!

Capt. Lougino left the battery today – he is to become a Major. First Lieut Schaiff is now in command.

McLandon is next and I'm the junior position.

"Four thousand miles from home and not a ship in sight - rain and cold - mud - war - France - Hell boys, let's go home!" March 31, 1918

JOHN LOCKE DOGGETT JR

4

April

Monday April 1

It looks as if I am about to move again – Major Gilmore is organizing two howitzer batteries (motorized) and since I've had work with tractors I'll be elected! I've now had the 155s long the 19s and 81 howitzer – and all in three months! This is either a great war or I'm a great officer!

Tuesday April 2

The Boche offensive has assumed planning proportions – the advance now will be approximately 50 kilometers – guess that's more than the allies have made in three years. More rain – cold and mud and no money – bed is the best place for me. Goodnight

Two soldiers stand with a 155m howitzer

A 155mm howitzer at an American base in France

Wednesday April 3

Lots of the same rain – mud – and I had the pleasant job of going out with the work gangs today so I feel just like the weather.

Thursday April 4

Bath night!

Friday April 5

Too cold for words

Saturday April 6

Orders received to break billets – back to Haussimont to-morrow. The Portuguese are to relieve us and we think we are slated for the Front! I have hated to leave our French family as the old folks are "gentle" even though they have a habit of "picking up" ones odds and ends.

A soldier takes a bath

Soldiers of the C.A.C bathe in a local river

Sunday April 7

We entrained at 9:30 and we rode to Vitry[16] and were side tracked there for five hours – spent all our money eating at British Red Cross so I could talk to a "peach" – she's typically British but yea boa! Vitry has recently been bombed by German avions. This particular "peach" told us she has to take to the cellar for safety. We arrived Soulosse-sous at 9:15 – marched three kilometers to Haussimont – bed at 12:30. It took us 12 hours to go thirty miles by train.

Capt. Lougino has rejoined us.

Monday April 8

Capt. Lougino had a talk with Col. Greig this morning and the word is I am to stay with the battery and we leave for the Front on Saturday – what luck, I'd rather be with the "19s" at the Front than train with the 8 inch Howitzers for the rest of the Summer! For an ignoramus I've created a fuss – both Captains are going and Lougino has been scraping for my valuable services and I don't know a thing!!!

Strong retreat tonight.

Back to the old routine.

Tuesday April 9

Reassigned officially to "H"

Leave for Front on Saturday.

Artillery drill all morning – Gas Mask inspection *après midi*[17]. We are checking up on equipment and personnel before our departure. We have received recruits today to be molded into a 4th gun section and a reserve section as we expect to lose some from casualties and gas since our sector is particularly active at present.

Wednesday April 10

Drilled our guns all morning – turned men loose early this afternoon for a ball game.

Thursday April 11

Checking on our equipment – drilled more on gas masks this AM. The respirators are unbearable after a couple of hours. We are told they are worn sometimes six to twelve hours up Front. Very difficult to make the men wear them properly.

Mail from Home today!

"Gas school has started and my eyes are opened to the task ahead of me – gas is the worst modern way to torture humans" - April 17, 1918

"The respirators are unbearable after a couple of hours. " April 11, 1918

"Very difficult to make the men wear them properly." April 11, 1918

Friday April 12

I have been appointed Battalion Gas Officer – HA! HA! But let it be said Gas is the deadliest weapon of the war. I'd like to duck my job; the responsibility will make my gray haired. I will take a week's training at W.S. Gas School and then form my battery.

Saturday April 13

More drill – we hoped to leave today but can't get our train made up – infantry inspections – also a cootie hunt. Though our 14 recruits brought home some bacon. We are boiling the clothes – must taste like Donac[18] soup, eh Momsey?!

Took retreat.

Sunday April 14

Left Haussimont

I have spent the entire day writing letters – under present conditions this is almost an impossible job.

It's Spring – by the calendar – but we still have slurs of mud – rain – wind.

We will not get away now until Tuesday or Wednesday – I have no further dope on the Gas – hope I've ducked it.

Monday April 15

Arrived Langres

After I had hit the bed last night, orders came in ordering me to gas school at Langres immediately. I left with Lt. Putt and his men at 6:15 AM today – having gotten up at 5:00

to pack! Travelled all day via Troyes arriving here (Langres) tonight.

This is a wonderful old place – situated on the summit of a high mountain, it is a typically walled city of olden times. More later – I'm dead to the world.

Tuesday April 16

No school today – I spent the day orienting myself.

I have no cot so I slept on the floor for a week. Food is plentiful in this little city – possibly this is due to the presence of so many Cols., Majors, and Generals. General Staff Headquarters are here. I shall not try to describe this town – it was built by the Romans and its limits are still marked by the huge stone walls running around the summit of the mountain.

From my windows I can see easily 30 miles in every direction – the Alps are visible on clear days.

Wednesday April 17

Gas school has started and my eyes are opened to the task

ahead of me – gas is the worst modern way to torture humans – a typical German method of fighting.

Our course will take one week and we shall study defensive measures only. The course is interesting solely for its gruesomeness and barbarity.

Thursday April 18

The more I learn of my duties as G.O the heavier I realize are my responsibilities – but sleep drives drill call away – Voila!

Friday April 19

Today I corralled my sergeant and four corporals and bawled 'em out on the work – then passed the buck and had them drill each other. We entered a chamber full of tear gas for testing purposes and I cried as if I were spanked.

I have no desire to try out the mustard gas. I find the English mask superiors to all other respirators. Where is our Yankee Genius?

This afternoon I walked around the parapet which

surrounds our city – this scenery beggars description and words fail me.

Saturday April 20

More Gas drills and lectures in the A.M.

This afternoon we drove 17 kilometers to the camouflage factory and demonstration grounds of the General Staff for observation of camouflage. The trip proved intensely interesting – trick trench – periscopes of barbed wired poles – faked trees – faked infantry men – hidden houses. I wish I was a lizard too!

To stimulate activity, we got balled up with some trench mortar men and came into their line of fire – several bombs landing entirely too near us. I've began to believe my War Risk insurance was a good investment!

Sunday April 21

Slept late – ate a late breakfast – had a real hot shower and shave.

Studied this afternoon at Y.M.C.A. Wrote Momsey and L.L

It snowed this morning!

Monday April 22

We attended lectures all day on offensive Gas – particular stress being laid on Liven's Projector[19] and Stokes Mortars.[20]

Tuesday April 23

Course finished – we receive instruction finally as to our duties. We examined our H.C.O's officially and report their grades. Packed up and caught Paris express for Troyes. Stayed there for the night – poor beds, poor eats – rain –

Wednesday April 24

Held over in Troyes until 5:00 P.M for transportation. Visited the Cathedral, but nothing yet can touch the Notre Dame for spectacularity.

Caught 5:00 train for Sommes Sous. The French Captain with his Legion of Honor-grey hair – war.

Arrived Sommes Sous – got breaks and rations for my men – reported my arrival at Headquarters. My battery is now at the Front.

Otis is in Mailly and I can't get to him and it's an absolute tragedy. I'd give my shirt to see him.

I hear there are many Italian at Mailly also.

Thursday April 25

Left at 2:30 P.M. in a truck with my men for the Front – I really consider this the biggest day I have had yet in France. The approach to the Front went something like this – Châlus presented the 1st signs of war – we ate at Red Cross Station – The town has recently been bombed by Avions. About two kilometers from Châlus we came to reserve Trenches and barbed wire entanglements.

Red Cross dressing stations – more Trenches – autos galore going to and from the Front. We found Suippes gutted but no shells dropped as we passed through – the road is serviced or camouflaged from the Boche. Arrived at Battery Camp. We live in dug outs – boarded up inside and bomb proofed. We are part of the 4th French Army – this is in the Argonne Forest. My camp is "3/5" – and my first night here was almost sleepless.

The flare of the guns and noise of the blasts is terrific – this is really war and I am now a veteran – **At The Front.**

Friday April 26

My Casualty Card is filled out! I am issued an anti-louse necklace but the smell almost makes the cooties preferable. I made a reconnaissance around the epis[21] – our camouflage is well done.

Everything has been quiet – only shell holes show what's been happening here. We are building our gas proof dugouts near the firing position. We wear our steel helmets as protection from shrapnel – and gas mask always slung over our shoulders. The French live entirely underground in the chalk – their dugouts are as deep as 15 meters.

Food is plentiful up here. We are five kilometers from the Boche trenches. Weather is very bad and observation impossible.

"About two kilometers from Châlus we came to reserve Trenches and barbed wire entanglements." - April 25, 1918

"The French live entirely underground in the chalk – their dugouts are as deep as 15 meters." - April 26, 1918

Saturday April 27

I slept like a top[22] last night despite the ratchet here abouts. Today I plotted the position of our Targets –got range – gradient – we are to do counter battery work.

A big pile of work for me today – word from home is marvelous and everyone is wonderful to me.

Capt. Lougino has been summoned to consult with Major Gilmore on an emergency call – he has been gone over one hour and I am waiting for him – there's big dope afloat – maybe!

The 155's and 3/20's are barking all around – the *poilu* loves to tease the Boche.

Capt. Lougino returned – his only comment was that our guns will be brought up tomorrow night and that we probably would not get back to Haussimont for many days. I think we are on the Front for the Summer.

Gas suits were issued today.

Monday April 29

We have almost finished our gas proof dug outs – they look more like dungeons. I have attempted to design a door of my invention to keep out gas.

I have omitted to mention activities here – the 155's are battling 'em out continuously – at least I cannot see again as observation is out of the question.

Tuesday April 30

Up all last night bringing the guns and ammunition trains into position and placing them under the camouflage. St. Hilaire – St. Etienne – Dampierre – Suippes – Camp 3/5.

JOHN LOCKE DOGGETT JR

5

May

Wednesday May 1

Today was fairly clear. Two French Generals have visited our positions and inspected our camouflage and pronounced it well-nigh perfect.

Capt. Lougino and I have rigged up a quoit[23] game.

Thursday May 2

I walked up to the nearest observation station to the German lines today and have my first good look at no man's land. The desolation is indescribable. Our position was again inspected by Col. Goethals of the engineers, a son of Gen Goethals. The weather is still clearing up – one or two observation balloons are up. The shelling by the French last night was thunderous. The machine guns in the trenches also spit continuously.

Friday May 3

Weather clear – hills still hazy. Saw an air bombardment for the first time – a Boche flew over our position and the 75's opened up on him – We paid off our men today.

I gave the *nou-couis*[24] a special talk on gas – the French seem to fear a Yperite[25] attack – we have taken all precautions. We expect to fire tomorrow. Schaiff has been ordered to headquarters as adjutant[26] leaving the Capt. for B.C. and Mac and I to take charge of the guns.

Saturday May 4

We received orders to open up at about 1.38. I was in care of guns 3 and 4, Mac taking 1 and 2. The sky was filled with aeroplanes – the Boche making desperate attempts to locate us – firing only to be driven back by French Barrages across the sky. Weather clear as crystal. This morning I inspected gas masks and held a drill – posted my gas sentries.[27]

We fired 100 shells from the 4 Guns. The men worked

splendidly – our balloon reported two hits and we were ranging on our second target when ordered to cease firing. Orders
received after supper to move guns off epis as French expect a
gas attack so we worked until 1:00 A.M.

Leaving the guns at 151. Terribly tired – but I've sent my
first messages to the Boche who did not respond a single time.
Our camouflage must really be excellent.

Sunday May 5

We find 100 shells – my guess sending 21 and 25 respec-
tively. Before firing I had to talk bull to a visiting French
Commander and six Portuguese officers. They were on a tour
of instruction and damn 'em they busted one of my gas
proof doors.

The Lafayette Escadrille[28] sent six airplanes up after the
Boches today and one enemy avion was shot down. Mac
moved our ammunition – guns and camouflage to position
209 tonight – evidently, we will not fire here again – Though
the Boche has not fired on us yet.

I wrote up my report of the firing – also our math cal-
culations in ranging on Boche battery. We are credited with
two hits.

A dog sits atop a German plane shot down by
Battery H

An enemy German plane shot down by Battery H

Monday May 6

Rest – weather bad – really the reason this War has lasted so long is that only about one-third of the days are fit for fighting.

Saw Legion of Honor presented to 16 men – about 20 Croix de Guerre[29] awarded 2 medals Militaire. Ceremony took place before a French regiment of infantry – and a troop cavalry – very impressive – especially the final review.

The fighting tonight in the front-line trenches seems to be particularly heavy – the Boche is hitting some of our nearby positions which are close enough to have each detonation shake my shack – that is close enough!

Tuesday May 7

More rain – was officially notified that I will now be Battalion Gas Officer in addition to my other duties! I thought I was in for something like this.

We dined with the officers of a French machine gun company tonight – a royal French meal – hors d'oeuvres, rabbit, peas, picard, salad, cakes, nuts, raisins, cheese, and champagne.

Things fairly quiet – guess the Fritzies[30] got enough last night.

A soldier rides his bike through flooded French land

Wednesday May 8

Foggy, damp – *c'est la France* but a generous mail from

home has sent my spirits to the proper place. We played bridge in the dug outs all day.

Thursday May 9

Col. Howell on General Staff came over to inspect our position, epis, etc – he seemed pleased, especially over the report of our shooting. Later he said that my battery fired the first heavy guns of the Americans against the Huns – it is justly famous.

Friday May 10

The Capt. went into Mailly today – leaving me in command of the battery and had my hands full. Major Gilmore ordered our aero drill with radio and panels and I had to act as B.C. and coordinate all movements – it's a hard life!

After the drill – I reported at headquarters – Cassidy, I, Major Gilmore and the interpreter drove with the French aviators then we went over our data. I returned home about 11:00 P.M.

Saturday May 11

I awoke to find myself a Battery Commander! Capt Gilmore was promoted to a Majorship – I went into his place temporarily. Had to sign ranging reports. Settled a wordy battle between a *nou-couis* and private by cussing out the latter. Instructed my radio sergeant, and Lance Corporal Furlong, on panels – helped answer mail, and conducted a drill with aero again. We are good!

Schaiff is coming back to take charge of Battery tomorrow. If I was only a 1st Lt they would have left me in command – but what chance has a poor "Shave-tail" got!

Sunday May 12

Schaiff came over and I'm now 2nd in command. I got permission to move into Mailly today by Murdoch – and saw Otis Bradley. It was like seeing my own brother – we talked and laughed. Finally, I had to don my tin hat and I'm back on the Front.

Monday May 13

Things have resumed their normal trend and routine. Nothing of importance, rather than hearing firing last night.

Tuesday May 14

The Portuguese are going to fire from our epis – I talking with their Porky[31] Capt. this morning. He is temperamental to his shoestrings.

Wednesday May 15

We were again inspected by the district French Major –

I am now mess officer – another 'fat' job! The Inspector General of the Artillery, Col. Matthews, will be over next week to inspect our battery – I've got to learn a hundred different ways to cook beans! The Portuguese have moved me to the epis.

Thursday May 16

I have been recommended for a promotion – great scott – what have I done. Doc Bernard scared me stiff when he bobbed up to give us a physical examination today – I think Col. Guig got my name mixed up with someone else's!

Rain and fog prevented the Portuguese from firing.

Friday May 17

The Portuguese fired this afternoon – torrential observation – the Capt. said it was wretched. They saw over 15 Salvos[32] from 4 guns – 60 shots in all. They were not very successful.

Saturday May 18

The Boche flew over early this morning to locate our Latin friends – but the bird had flown. This afternoon I observed 150 fire from cote 200 – I am going up to the front-line trench first opportunity – ought to know what sort of life the dough boy leads.

Sunday May 19

Captain Garduier has returned and is assigned to our battery – I'm not too proud of him – he is a solo dancer! But had a high stand at the H.A.S

Monday May 20

Sunday I entered the 1st line trenches – and have paid dearly for it too. We walked through three miles of sun baked trenches then tunnels etc – finally we came to this position

The "X" indicates a cleverly arranged observation post – from here I could almost have thrown pebbles into the Boche and he had never discovered this position. The dots indicate machine guns – 4 – very cleverly camouflaged and only reached after going down a long tunnel and up to a tiny opening in the ground. We are introduced the Major of this position and drank some French coffee with him. Our guide was a captain of the machine guns Co (French) which held the position above. I asked him to take us up – He thought I was crazy – but only a few shots were fired – it was too hot to fight – but I've seen the Boche in his den.

140

Monday May 20

Saturday I entered the 1ˢᵗ line
trenches and have paid
dearly for it too. We walked
through three miles of sun baked
trenches then tunnels etc —
finally we came to this position.
The X indicates a
cleverly arranged observation
post — from here I could
almost have thrown pebbles into the
Boche and he had never discovered
this position. The dots indicate machine
guns — 4 — very cleverly camouflaged. and only reached after going
down a long tunnel and up to a
tiny opening in the ground. We
were introduced the Gun Major
of this position and drank
some trench coffee with him
Our guide was a Captain of
the Machine Gun Co (French) which
held the position above. I asked
him to take us up — the thought
I was crazy — but only a
few shots were fired — it was
too hot to fight — but I've seen
the Boche in his den.

Page from the original Terminal Diary - May 20,
1918

Tuesday May 21

I said I paid dearly for my trip – I did – I caught trench fever – sort of grippe and chills – rotten – had fever for three days – sure wished for home and my two sweethearts –

The life of the dough boy up there is pitiful – he is on duty for seven days in front lines – they never sleep nights and someone is watching and waiting every minute of the day. They sleep under muddy steel trees – in muddy Abris – any place where they can. The strain must be hardly durable. I saw no real cooties but there was competitive scratching!

Wednesday May 22

Still on sick list – "I want to go home" Wonderful mail today.

Was told that Châlus is full of British coming up to our Front. This is new dope.

Thursday May 23

The Boche has flown over our position for the last three

mornings and the French have been showering the skies with shrapnel – the Boche must be a suspicious rascal – we've got him fixed.

Tomorrow I take some *blaireau*[33] exam in Trig. I may have to go through the H.A.S now – I've ducked it twice.

Friday May 24

Feeling O.K. – no news except rain –

Saturday May 25

We are soon to start epis work. French near us were gassed last night – nothing has disturbed us yet.

Sunday May 26

Today the Boche resumed his great offensive, started May 21st. I am forty miles south of the southern end of the drive. We shall now watch the Kaiser hang himself.

Monday May 27

No duties – today the Boche sent over propaganda balloons – I have one of the newspapers – written in French.

"Today the Boche sent over propaganda balloons" -
May 27, 1918

Tuesday May 28

To Châlus for the day with McClandon – we had a splendid feed at Hotel Augustine – there are many Englishmen there – Back to camp to find the Boche shelling ammunition dumps in our rears! The Frogs are answering and we are in the midst of the duel. Think I shall sleep with my Gas Mask handy tonight.

Wednesday May 29

My orderly called us at 6:00 AM reporting that we must fire as soon as possible.

Amazed – I dressed – found the guns has been brought up on the epis. We worked hard and were ready to fire by 2:00 PM. The wind was too high – we waited until 3:30 PM.

No firing till tomorrow – our objective is the Boche battery which yesterday fired on Suippes.

Thursday May 30

I've opened fire at 8:00 AM and fired 194 rounds – my gun fired 49 out of a possible 51. We annihilated our target. This was a fitting way to celebrate Decoration today.

Friday May 31

Informal muster. I went over to the guns to give verbal report to our *Groupement* Commander (French) and I show breakage. Repairs are going to be made immediately – new ammunition arrives tonight. The Boche drive is reported to be nearing the Marne – this seems incredible. We may be cut off from Paris.

JOHN LOCKE DOGGETT JR

Portraits

Portraits of WWI Soldiers in the Army Coast Artillery Corps, Battery H/E

635
AM
ELD   SER
GE MAXIMA
COUCHES
OU 4 ASSIS

AMBULANCE
S.S.U. N° XVII
35607
AM

June

Monday June 1

The major (Lougino) takes charge of the group today and will drive to Headquarters. The Dutchman has reached our side of the Marne – the R.R^{34} believes Châlus AND Paris is destroyed – we are perfecting plan to draw rations from the French – our lines of communication are almost to be cut off.

Sunday June 2

Last night or rather this morning at 3:00 AM the gas alert woke us – the Boche got fresh. The battery behaved splendidly. Major Lougino has left us.

Everything quiet today.

Monday June 3

Up to the Front again for observation with 75's. The French were shelling a Boche communication trench. I've had tea with the French officers and returned home at dark. The French have removed practically all their infantry – we are open to the Boche.

Tuesday June 4

Our position continues to be more precarious – the Boche is now to the southwest of us – we are cut off from Paris for fair – all artillery is moving out.

Wednesday June 5

This morning I sent all my men through a Gas chamber – tested and examined all masks. This PM attended a conference with the French in a new fuse – to correct fire by bursts.

Thursday June 6

In to Mailly – saw Otis – got a cot at last. Everybody very

sober over outlook. Returned to find that Boche have again been shelling our camp – two French were killed. We fire at 7:00 AM in the morning – rise at 4:00am. Boche avions early this morning flew over our position again – shrapnel fell over my dugout.

The road from Châlus to Mailly was peppered with refugees and fleeing civilians – this is one of the saddest sights to be seen. I regard our situation here as serious – we have no protection but fight we shall.

"The road from Châlus to Mailly was peppered with refugees and fleeing civilians - this is one of the saddest sights to be seen. " - June 6, 1918

Friday June 7

Ho – what a day! Up at 4:00 AM – ready to fire at 7:00 am. The Boche after our third salvo made desperate efforts to locate us and two thrilling air fights took place. We fired from 7:30 AM to 2:15 PM without rest. 370 rounds – 80 salvos – a new record in the French army for 19's!

Three American majors visited our battery for the firing – also a German spy in the uniform of a French Lieutenant – he escaped – the French are searching the woods as he has full information of our battery, personnel etc. Plus – some-one – we haven't found the culprit – ripped our gas curtains to shreds – had them repaired at 4:30 AM and have reported the outrage to Headquarters. Better news from the rest of our front today – the line is holding. *Bon Soir*

Saturday June 8

Our guns were moved back to the edge of the gas zone again – I was up and down on the epis with Major Lougino, Major Arman and Mac – an examination of our time fuse setter showed we had been improperly instructed in its use and Major L raised Hell. Everyone is proud of the Battery's excellent firing

Sunday June 9

No rest for the weary!

My Sunday morning extra hours sleep was lost – I had to hurry down to the guns with Mac and two gun crews to have sight there – also to send all parts needing repairs to the "base hospital" for guns. In the afternoon the battery lost its first baseball game. I stayed on duty here and wrote letters then Lt. Ferralli (or what-not) and I swapped yarns and in the end he presented me with a young rabbit. More work for Woodie. Rabbit is dubbed "Minnie" but I am not yet convinced as to whether this name is entirely appropriate. Rabbit gender is an uncertain affair.

The landscape of the Mailly region of France

"In the afternoon, the battery lost its first baseball
game." - June 9, 1918

Monday June 10

We have had no mail for two days – absolutely only those
things which are essential are being delivered to the armies –

food and ammunition and for the French wine, wine, wine they must bathe in it.

Rats are about to oust me from my dug out – they and the incessant bombardments of 155's – make the night a burden. Oh for home sweet home.

I've had a pistol match with Capt. Vincent, Lts. Verdit, Durandi and Le Docteur. The latter won – I came second, Mac third. I beat Mac and he's from Texas – so I'm content

Tuesday June 11

Had to refuse our invitation to Mailly with Major L. for the day as I can't leave the guns until the French return the repaired parts. However, Capt. Garduier and I scooted over to St. Reims for green vegetables.

I learned that a new division of French will move in shortly on our sector. Thank heavens for kind favors – we will now be strongly entrenched – but why this sudden move – will the West drive come this way?

Last night the Germans shelled Suippes again – we will undoubtedly fire as soon as our guns are repaired.

Wednesday June 12

Rewarded our kitchen – moved the battery into the open during meal hours – this solves the fly problem. Drilled more with respirators for one hour – made a baseball diamond alongside our epis with Gas masks on!

At eleven fifteen tonight the Boche rudely roiled us from sleep with gas shells – we were forced to wear masks for 13 hours and a half. Men behaved splendidly – no casualties. We boiled eggs for safety sake – the gas officer is a thankless title to hold – no sleep tonight.

Great mail today – 19 letters.

Thursday June 13

Aired all equipment to clear of gas – established definitive dues on entry into abris.

Boche routed us out again – 10:30 PM – with gas – the "all clear" sounded at midnight. Guess the Dutchman don't like us – we shoot too damn straight. I have been up now since Tuesday morning – no sleep – tis a great war. Bah!

Friday June 14

Capt. Garduier sent us into Châlus on battery missions so I had a bit of a rant – was glad to lift a load off my chest for a while. Bought screens for kitchen – green vegetables – and 2 picture frames for my two best girls – Reddie and Momsey!

Back in time to dine with French officers – farewell food – liked the eats but not enough water!

No gas – praise Pete.

Saturday June 15

Major Lougino inspected the battery – I was O.D. – he was pleased with conditions. Mac has been made supply officer. Schaiff and Garduier are at "outs" – I'm trying to be cupid!

Wrote on my firing report.

Sunday June 16

Letters to all the folks at home.

Don't think Schaiff will last long if we continue to be undiplomatic with the Capt.

| 146 |

Monday June 17

Received firing order – we worked late computing the data – our target are crossroads – and important depots opposite – we are to have an observation – seems a queer procedure.

Tuesday June 18

O.D. took inspection.

Guns are to come up tomorrow.

Our Y M.C.A friends failed to appear at this post as well – we should not have entertained them.

Wednesday June 19

Six "casuals" were shoved on to us for a week's visit at the Front – observing.

I laid out Points P for our 5 targets

Schaiff brought up the guns tonight.

Thursday June 20

Set up 12 aiming rules – an all-day job!

Maj. Hardaway tonight served us evacuation orders. The dope is that the Boche is going to start his next push right through us! Our sector offers a rational path to enter and flanks Reims. We are to fire until ammunition is gone or until Boche pushes us out – what property we cannot save will be destroyed

Friday June 21

We are all ready to fire – have perfected evacuation plans but we are going to fight 'em to a standstill first. We are the only Railway artillery in this sector and have no support. Every man has been issued 100 rounds of ammunition – baggage was loaded today in Rly cars. Commandant Lambert inspected our position and pronounced it perfect. Weather is bad.

Saturday June 22

Everything calm with us which is not to my liking. I'd rather bust things up a bit than deliberately wait for the Boche to push through. Watchful waiting is bad for the digestion – we have no news.

Sunday June 23

Artillery activity heavy around Riems – with us only June showers! But we know huge supplies are daily being accumulated by the Germans in camps opposite us.

Monday June 24

A French *coup de' maine* gave 4 Boche prisoners the report – large concentration of troops opposite us – wish they'd let us open fire.

Schaiff relieved from duty with this battery – I am not surprised.

Tuesday June 25

We were paid off today –

Casuals left –

"Ogive" came to fill Schaiff's place – he is a good scout.

Doc Felt has joined us.

Wednesday June 26

A few of our men crowded trenches with Booze – they are now doing hard labor!

The battery went through the gas number this morning

Thursday June 27

Mac has arrived – welcome home!

We walked up to cote 200 but everything is deadly quiet.

We are being reinforced with 155's and 75's and infantry reserves are arriving – Praise Peter.

Six months ago, today I sailed from NY.

Friday June 28

Was, at my request, relieved as Mess officer. Mauhart has taken my place and I became R.R officer – this means more night work but it's more agreeable.

Saturday June 29

Capt. scooted to Châlus on business – so of course something had to happen. Two American Generals dropped in on us – Ogive and I did the honors and handed out a line of bull which was swallowed whole – said, Generals being on their first visit at the Front! But they had heard of "H" Battery – *c'est assez.*[35]

Sunday June 30

Fillibert – Major *du coup.*

Reported that Boche aviators last night landed in our vicinity, we burned their machines and disappeared! Therefore, we have placed a strong guard around our guns – I am O.D.

This morning a "Frog" in our camp was killed by falling anti-aircraft shrapnel – huge chunk fell immediately to the rear of my dug out but I slept peacefully! What we don't know about don't hurt.

JOHN LOCKE DOGGETT JR

8 |

July

Monday July 1

Rain – *rieu de tout!*

Tonight, I got away for a few hours – drove thirty-five kilo-meters to hear an American band - all negroes with Europe as leader[36] – Oh boy – to hear those old "rags"[37] once more.

Tuesday July 2

Officer of the day – inspected guard at 10:30 am – 2:30 PM – 8:00 PM, 1.4 JA.M[38] and 9:30 AM.

Everything clear but heavy artillery action to the east of us, a car passed by marked aero-plane activities – our camo was littered with shrapnel.

General weekly inspection of gas equipment.

Durandi and Vincent visited us today.

"Reported that Boche aviators last night landed in our vicinity, we burned their machines and disappeared! " - June 30, 1918

Wednesday July 3

Thieves! Woody caught a Frog in my shack and one in his. They escaped! I persuaded the Capt. of a French land to give us a caucus tomorrow to celebrate the '4th" – provided the Boche behaves – I've a hunch he is going to be nasty just because it is the 4th.

Thursday July 4

The Americans are coming! The rainbow Division arrived this morning. More still to come. The blue devils are already on the line in front of us. French Batteries rattled through the night. I worked until 2:30 AM setting up aiming rules for 3 new targets. Just assigned a sharp *coup de main* by the French early in the evening, bought the big scrap a better plan but we are prepared – the Boche won at Aurieus Sorssieus[39] and Chateau Thierry – but he'll never break through us now, we are too strong.

No music today – work.

Iowa, Minnesota, Indiana troops are with us.

Friday July 5

Thousands of men – guns – horses, wagons continue to come up despite the failure of the Boche to come last night – perhaps the drive will start tonight – but who cares? Things will go along as usual – Major Harding dropped in for inspection – he's raising a fuss about all 34 SBRs[40]. The rainbow crowd are becoming disagreeable from the colonel down. Col. Aimett has appropriated the only abris we have on the hill for our office – said it was no place for men– but wait till an attack comes – we'll show him.

10:45 PM a sharp barrage to our right brought orders from St. Remy to open up – we fired all night supported by many batteries of 155's.

Saturday July 6

[The number"169" is written atop the page]

The noise was terrific and fireworks display showing Paris finest. Our objective was cross roads in St. Marie a Pry and Sommes Py. Ceased firing at 4:30 AM day eight. Pushed guns under camouflage – and growled for hot coffee. No shells fell our way – we have yet to lose a man.

Sent in firing reports to Americans and French head-quarters.

We had conferences with French – air plane observation reported gear damage done to enemy by our guns. Voila! Slept from 3 P.M. until 8AM.!

Sunday July 7

Everything comparatively quiet – our guns are cleaned - tracks repaired. The battery has a chicken and rabbit feed today. These rarities we bought from refugees – the first we've had.

We now have overflowing wild animals – we are a zoo! 1 cat – 4 kittens – 4 rabbits – 1 dog – 1 dead Magpie and Aggie has a pet cootie! Why worry about war when have such family hobbies as persuading said rabbits to become friendly with said dog.

Monday July 8

Mac came over and I hooked a ride to Châlus. First day off I've had in a month – spent all my money! I really had no business leaving the battery at such a critical moment but – got away with it!

Returned to find that we were to fire at 10:00 PM. We fired all night – layed off at 4:00 AM. Cleaned guns – off to sleep at 5:00. Woody awakened me with orders from headquarters to take a physical exam for protection. What the Doctors is up – this has happened twice before.

Saw Dick Wilson in Châlus – t'was great to see the old boy.

Tuesday July 9

Wrote up reports – repaired epis – slept – we are all up tonight waiting for orders to fire. The dope is that the Boche isn't coming here. We are stronger than at any time during the war – maybe the batteries know this and are going to strike elsewhere. The French are a bit worried –have they been out-witted?

Wednesday July 10

Back into Châlus on battery business i.e., eggs!

Col. Young, our new regimented commander, visited us today – and left a good impression.

Was ordered to take another physical exam for precautions – what the ____!

Thursday July 11

Made a belated inspection of gas masks and listed prizes.

Major Hardaway got excited over an order given us via phone from Headquarters and ruffled my feelings – I reported to headquarters and showed him that I was right and located the problem in his own headquarters.

The Iowa boys have been under shows orders – the frogs are worried again.

Friday July 12

Capt. Vincent, and Chiffonier called Durandy a pessimist for believing that the Boche must drive through us. The enemy must take the rest of Reims to get to Paris and we are on the driver road – come ahead Dutchies!

Durandy urges a diplomatic offensive by the French vs the Austrians – then in two months a mammoth French-American-British Offensive

Saturday July 13

O.D. – inspection of ground and quarters. Capt Garduier is at Châlus – with Nowlin. I see Jessie Robinson my good friend en route from NY to Mailly is dead. Poor Roby –

Later – two new targets and orders to fire at 5:00 AM – called Fisher over and set up rules on our position. When all ready – ordered to fire on old position and all rules had to be erased – all ready to fire – then – orders re'd no firing tonight and had to change back to new positions again – it is now 2:30 AM and we fire at 5:00! Nice night!

Sunday July 14

["124-" "81-" and "6/2" is written atop the page]

We were ready at 5:15 but musty weather made observation impossible – we stood around until 10 AM. Fired 120 rounds and demolished our enemy battery. New orders received at lunch to fire on Somme Py R.R Station – very poor observation but no. 4 guns hit Reservation pile causing huge explosion.

Sergeant Whalen and I heard the gun headquarters said "excellent". It's reported officially that the Boches are amassing for tonight. Despite delays the offensive seems sure to come. Let's hope not tonight – we all need sleep.

Some days later –

Here is what happened –[41]

At 10:45 am we were awakened by a terrific barrage of shrapnel; our quarters and camp became a checker board for shells. Hurriedly dressed, then came the gas. Worked my way to the battery and called for a volunteer to go to the epis with me, Houson stepped forward and by quick action we reached epis safety. The shrapnel bursts all around lighting up the way. At no. 3 epis the only phone line has been out by a shell fire and we could not reach the BC – we were forced to shelter and waited for orders. At 11:30 Ogive reached us with word of fire immediately – it was a different job to put guns in positions under a seething gas and shrapnel fire. The men worked wonderfully. I soon found there were many missing. I went to no. 3, got it firing with help of Nowlin. Then went to no. 4. Whalen was struggling along with half a gun section and no telephonic communications. Hansen, Bell, Wood, Notistine and others were exhausted. I played Powder Monkey[42] and fired the piece to hell. We worked this way the rest of the time. I was lucky – had only 2 misfires with the tankard. When daylight came the Boche shifted from gas and shrapnel to 150's and high explosives but they were off to the right 1007" in deflection. The shells hitting many horses and scattered dough boys. At sun up Boche Avions came over – 12 to 14 at a time – they shot down a French balloon war near us and then turned their machine guns on us. The Boche soon covered their fire and we were shelled with a deadly aim and our hit of wounded commander – I sent Woody to the BC for orders as to what to do when ammunition was exhausted - he never returned. Sent Bassitt next and he returned wounded without having reached Capt. Garduier. I sent Jones – he never returned – so at 10 AM when we used up all our ammunition – I ordered the guns put in traveling position and pushed to the mouth of the epis – this was a lucky move as no. 4 epis was next. Blown-up – then more men were wounded doing this. I found Jones had reached the Capt. and had been sent to gas the engine – we sent him to the mouth of the epis and pulled all guns out safely. Looking back at our old position we realized the great concentration of fire the men had worked under. I got Sergeant Green and went back to find the Captain. We got there alright and found the Capt. in the B.B – Woody has been wounded in 5 places, but we hope not seriously. The camp was far from the beautiful fine picnic grounds of 24 hours before. A shell had struck my dugout and smashed it to pieces. I found Woody had saved most of my stuff – including this poor diary. There were many dead around the shack – I remember one Frenchman lying under a dead horse. His arms and one leg shot off and head crushed in. Many men from the Iowa infantry had been killed but the line had held – the Boche never gained a foot - the first time his offensive had failed. Our men had fired for 30 hours – 12 being under gas and high explosives. We lost 15 wounded. We took our men and train to Dauphine au Temper to rest.

195

Sunday July 14

we were ready at 5:15 but misty weather made observation impossible — We stood around 'till 10 a.m. fired 12 rounds & demolished our enemy battery. Unit orders received at lunch to fire on same by R.R. Station — very poor observation but No 4 gun hit ammunition pile causing huge explosion. Sig. Whalen & I had the gun & Hdgrs said "Excellent!" It is reported officially that the Boches are massing men for tonight — Despite delays the offensive seems sure to carry. Let hope not tonight — we all need Sleep.

Some days later —
Here is what Happened —
At 10.45 we were awakened by a terrific barrage of Shrapnel, our quarters & camp became a charnel bound for shells. Humanly during. Then came the gas. Worked my way to the Battery & called for a volunteer to go to the spur with me. Hanson

Page from the original Terminal Diary - July 14, 1918

Monday July 15

stepped forward - & by quick action we reached
this early - the shrapnel bursts all around
lighting up the way. At No 3 epi the only phone
line had been cut by shell fire & we could not
reach the B.C. - we were forced to shelter & waited
for orders. At 11.30 ~~guns~~ reached up with
used to fire immediately - it was a difficult job
to put guns in position ~~with~~ under a withering gas
& shrapnel fire - the men worked wonderfully
I soon found there were many missing.
~~toward~~ I went to No 3 got it firing
with help of Nowlin. Then went to No 4
Whalen was struggling along with half
a gun section & no telephonic communication
Hanson, Bell, wood, Notestine & others were
exhausted. I played Powder Monkey &
fired the piece to help. We worked this
way the rest of the time - I was
lucky & had only 2 misfires with
the Lanyard. When day light came the
Boche shifted from gas & shrapnel to
150's & high explosives but they were
off to the right, 100 yds in deflection. the shells
killing our own horses & scattered doughboys.
At sun up Boche avions came over - 12 to
14 at a time - they shot down a French
balloon near us & then turned their

Page from the original Terminal Diary - (continued)
July 14, 1918

machine guns on us. The Boche soon
corrected their fire & we were shelled
with a deadly aim & our list of wounded
commenced — I sent Woody to the B.C.
for orders as to what to do when ammunition
was exhausted — he never returned. Sent Bassett
next & he returned wounded without having
reached Capt Gordon. I sent Torres — he
never returned — So at 10. A.M. when
we had used up all our ammunition — I ordered the guns put in travelling position &
pushed to the mouth of the epi — this was a
lucky move as No 4 epi was next blown
up — then more men were wounded doing
this. I found Torres had reached the Capt & had been
sent to get the engine — we met him at the mouth of
the epis & pulled all guns out safely. Looking
back at our old position we realized the
great concentration of fire the men had worked
under. I got Sug. Gish & went back to find the
Capt — we got there alright & found the Capt in
the B.C. — Woody had been wounded in 5 places,
but we hope not seriously. The camp was far
from the beautiful pine picnic ground 72
hours before. A shell had struck my dug
out & smashed it to pieces — I found
Woody had saved most my stuff — including

A soldier lies dead after the Second Battle of the
Marne

A man lies dead in a trench as two American
soldiers overlook the destruction

"There are many dead around the shack." - July 14, 1918

Tuesday July 16

Capt Garduier sent me to headquarters to report – to get there I had to pass through Suippes and St. Remy and got more of a chance to see what damage the Boche had done. These villages were still being shelled by big guns. Reported to Major Hardaway – he was immensely pleased with our showing. I reported back to commander Lambert and he declared the Battery had displayed venerable noble courage and grit to stick on the job! I set out next to find our wounded and traced McKinsy and Woodward to alive. Woody had just been operated on and I think he was mighty glad to see me – I gave him 50 franks and McKinsy 30. Two men – named

Linton and Wallace are lost – we have no trace of them. No gas causalities.

Wednesday July 17

Thoroughly inspected all gas equipment which has suffered much damage. Went back to our old position with 20 men to pick up 32 shells we had left because the powder had been blown up. The stench from dead horses was terrific – the camp was still under intense fire but nothing struck us. Returned to find the Boche Avions trying to bomb our train but their aim was poor.

Thursday July 18

Rested all day. At supper we received orders to go back to old position and open fire on Boche at 6:00 AM. Our objective being a long-range battery. I was ahead to orient the aiming rules. Found the French in possession of all our dug outs – had to drive 'em out of our own P.C. The train came up at midnight. We worked all night and were ready to fire at six.

Friday July 19

[The number "50" is written atop the page]

No Frenchie aviators showed up until 7:45 and we opened fire. Its suicide to bring our ruin back but we banged away and Boche Avions began to become inquisitive. Some Frogs showed up and we saw a lively air battle. The poor frogs came down – but the French made up by bringing down a Boche balloon. Things must have become too hot for our observer because [he] landed and we had to cease firing. We lounged around all day waiting for another observer but none showed up – then this wind turned and the stench from a hundred or more decayed horses was terrific. We returned to the train on position 151 and slept – the first we had had in another 36 hours.

We have been told that the battery has been cited before the Army and some of us have been recommended for Croix de Guerre – including myself.

Saturday July 20

We stayed in position 151 all day somewhat exposed to avion's machine gun fire and at night bombs were dropped but none hit near enough to do damage. Capt. Vincent turned up with 10 kilos of honey.

Sunday July 21

Major Hardaway came over to bull around.

Also four cars of ammunition came in and give one an uncertain feeling when the avions prowl around.

I understand artillery fire around the epis makes things uncomfortable but we are resting today.

Monday July 22

I went through the old camp again – what a sad sight! Have photographed my ruined shack and nearby shell holes.

Tuesday July 23

Because of our exposed position at 151 we moved to Poste A – two kilometers back but we're now sleeping alongside a loaded bridge – a target for Avions – it's a great life!

Commandant Quade looked us over and agreed that life in ammunition cars is not healthy so we will be installed in barracks – they look infested with cooties etc. but I'd rather scratch than shiver!

Paid off the men.

Wednesday July 24

Received 100 new Tissot[43] masks for the battery as a result of my letter to Headquarters.

Frenchies accused some of our men of stealing 1500 francs – and we had to make a dirty investigation but our men seemed to be innocent and we finally had to tell the Frogs to go to hell.

Thursday July 25

We could not move to new barracks because the Howitzer regiment is resting there for the day. Issued the Tissots and instructed the men in their use.

Mail from home – AH!

A Red Cross ambulance travels through the snow to
reach wounded soldiers.

A Red Cross ambulance with a damaged tire on the side of the road.

Friday July 26

We moved today – barracks were a mess. Aggie sent me to Mailly with the Doc to get "dope" to kill the cooties which the Frogs left behind. I stopped off in Châlus and let the Doc go to Mailly while I did some shopping. Châlus has changed, the avions have bombed it considerably.

My new quarters are very acceptable but offers no protection against the night raids – however we have learned to take these as a matter of course.

Our new camp is named Nantivet (Somme Suippes).

Saturday July 27

The whole day spent in getting located – the battery has a huge job on its hands cleaning up the filth. I was able to look up Durandy and swiped my cot – the boob was sleeping on it!

Avions encore.

Sunday July 28

Commandant Quade looked in on us informally and told the camp major we must be touted as the guests of France and every country that was given the Americans.

The battery is now well equipped with dugouts – I've had sneezing gas thrust upon us this afternoon by Fritz – nothing serious and really, it's funny to see every one cha-chowing including yourself.

Monday July 29

Major Benson – Brigade Engineer and gas officer came in

from Mailly. I gave him an oration on actual conditions we have to work under with gas and found out he was impressed. A very good old scour[44]. I took him up to see our epis and when he came to one place with 15 shell holes in a space of less than twenty feet he agreed that we have been working under trying conditions and decided he had seen enough when a few shells began dropping into the 155's about 400 meters north of us!

Tuesday July 30

Aggie and I betook ourselves to the brook for another bath – I proved myself a genius – the bottom of the creek being too soft to hold my weight so I confiscated an old bed frame and laid it on the bottom and I layed on top much to the envy of poor Aggie who fell into the brook while gazing at avions in all his nature's own gift.

I emphasize Baths – they are important incidents in our lives.

The Boche bound up at two tonight. No one but a few wagons blown up.

Wednesday July 31

Gas drill this morning on changing from S/B/R/'s to Tissot.

Mail from home gave me the distressing news that my commission as 1st is languishing in a frame in the den! I investigated at headquarters and will have to wait and show the papers!

Paele told me we had been uncovered for army corps citations with our Croix de Guerre – this would allow us to wear a palm too which is a high honor I am informed. Aggie tried to kid me about a D.S.C[45] but I refused to swallow his bait.

More bombs tonight.

9

August

Thursday August 1

Col. Young and Major Hardaway made a formal inspection of our new quarters – main complaint – dirty towels! Our superior officers have fine jobs – their line of criticizing is stereotyped. Thank heavens I'm not a major.

The Avions was never more successful. They hit a large ammunition dump which blew up with a flash that must have been seen for miles.

Friday August 2

Into Châlus with Aggie – we bummed around in the rain and didn't do much more than get wet. Back to the battery –

found our epis had been shelled a bit and two Frogs killed by gas.

No Avions tonight – praise be!

Saturday August 3

The Boche started in over the RR Station at Suippes today and shot up the team – we eat our due proportion – our man, Leine, was wounded rather badly. Not much gas tonight. There is some shelling but more to our right

Have had no word from Woody since he was evacuated from Auve.[46]

Sunday August 4

Major Lloyd came out and took all our finger prints.

General Paloqui adjutant to Gen. Herr – Chief of all France's heavy artillery came in today. I had the pleasure of showing him our position which he immediately said was too exposed. He plans to turn a new line in on us – place platforms under our guns thereby gaining all round fire and giving us the protection of the woods at the same time.

Aggie saw Capt. Vincent Durandy at La Cheppe.

Monday August 5

Due to heavy rain, the day was exceptionally quiet. A few shells fell near our B.C. car but we maintained communication without difficulty.

Pricella goes on leave tomorrow – she is SO excited!

Tuesday August 6

Aggie sprung an inspection on me this morning so I had play O.D! Major Hardaway came over with reorganizing our laws. Tonight, at midnight we became Battery E 42nd Arty CAC with headquarters as goal! The Famous "H" will now be no more. I have a new car – found her peacefully asleep in an old shell hole and she's a fine cat!

216

Sunday Aug 4

Page from the original Terminal Diary - August 4, 1918

French children carry a recently slaughtered hog

Wednesday August 7

Battery H is no more – our famous organization has lost its H – 150 long live 8!

Little of interest occurred today to relieve the monotony of the rain – I'm off to bed.

Thursday August 8

The sun deigned to shine on us and we were immediately given firing orders. I chased up to the epis with the battery – did my observation with Fisher – stalked the tracks and set up the aiming rule. Chased all frogs out of our dugouts but I fear the cooties remained behind.

We have located quite a number of nice German batteries – our objective is a battery of 77's. While at work shrapnel fell on our position and a large piece went through the top car narrowly missing 100lbs of dynamite. We fire at 7:00 AM tomorrow, weather permitting aerial observation.

Friday August 9

The weather did not permit – the visibility was rotten – so I went to St. Elain for 32 roulettes 5 Tn for the bores of the guns. Had a letter from Woody today – he is in Lyons with the French and reports his wounds are almost OK. I am mailing him socks etc. The allies have been making wonderful progress and now the British have started a push. I expect to see the Boches on the defensive from now on.

"Minnie's" wife lulu presented us with six splendid baby rabbits today – all are doing nicely thank you. Minnie has been caged to curtail his animalistic instincts and Lillian, our antiquated duck, has quacked in glee at this dole violation of the proud daddy.

Saturday August 10

Weather still rotten – a high wind and low clouds makes things unprofitable. We will fire on the first clear day.

Fritzie fired on our camp this evening – dropped exactly 5 shells in rear of us and then quiet. Have been bulling with Serg Nowlin tonight, listening to his experiences in the Philippines, Japan, Mexico. Very interesting.

Sunday August 11

The clouds were still heavy but we tried it out at 6:30 this evening. The Boche would not allow our aviator to get near enough to observe so after 8 salvos we called it off. It was fire at will as we had no sooner left for home. The fritz opened up on us with shrapnel. Later on, during the night, he sent over about forty 105's but did no material damage.

Monday August 12

We finished our fire this morning – only a few shrapnel pouring from the Boche. We were very successful and served our objective. Commandant Quade was especially pleased. Last night the Boche shelled our epis – no casualties – part of no. 3 regle was hit and broken off.

Tuesday August 13

The French aviators came over after lunch and declared our firing the finest they had seen and have requested us to shoot with them again. We are ready. Major Hardaway also butted in and Aggies was in Châlus so I paraded up to the position – it is fitted with huge shell hole. The Major left and when he returned he cooked worries. Le Gare de Suippes was shelled this evening.

4A flag for the volunteer American Ambulance field service. SSU is French for "Section Sanitaire Unis" with 'Unis' indicated United States

Wednesday August 14

St. Remy has ordered us to fire again – I have reset the aiming rules – we are ready. The route to the epis was on the edge of a heavy artillery duel which I enjoyed watching immensely – from the size of the German bursts I imagine there to have been 105's.

I have actually had to quit smoking again. Gun trunks, as

per orders, will be stored in Mailly tomorrow. I fear this is the last I shall see of my outfit knowing the D.M. as I do.

Thursday August 15

Ogive and I went into Châlus – Aggie came in at lunch at the Renaud and told Ogive he had been ordered to the station – Glory what a surprise! Aggie left for the battery tout de suite[47]. We played around Châlus – saw Biddlesou.

Came "home" long route via St. Remy – arrived at Battery to find we were firing at 5:00 PM – so we went straight to the position. At six our aviator reported visibility so poor that firing was postponed until 6:00 AM tomorrow.

Friday August 16

[The numbers "160, 60, 90" are written atop the page]

We opened fire at 6:30 AM. – Fritzys were especially active and continually fired on our aviator. Our guns were not adjusting quickly and we did not start firing for effect until 8:30. Then all of a sudden, a big shell whizzed by and fell 30 yards to the rear of no. 3. The gas alarm was given and I revoked it after making the customary test. More shells, 150's and 77s, came piling over and it was plain the Germans were out to destroy our guns at any cost – Aggie gave orders to pull out guns – cease firing and sent me for the engine. Georer and I ducked down four big ones and managed to reach the motorcycle. Mauhart and Aggie directed the men and the guns were easily pushed to safety – not a man was hit. Direct hits on no. 1 dugout, no. 1 epis and no. 3 trench. I got to engine , found Ogive had taken auto cross country and beat me to it – then I saw the guns were rolling along pushed by the whole battery! Some luck! Immediately went back to epis, Aggie en route and was relieved to find him safe, epis were still being shelled. I found two men and sixteen horses.

Came back at 12 with Serg. Nowlin to chuck up our projectors and the damn Dutchmans repeated the operations – we had to take to the dugout. Went back in the afternoon with Fisher only to find shells still dropping – after a bit they stopped and we inspected the position – poor epis! Our firing position is undoubtedly the most exposed place in this sector.

228

Friday Aug 16

We opened fire at 6 30 A.M. - Fritz's Archies were especially active and continually fired on our aviators. Our guns were not adjusting quickly and we did not start firing for effect until 8. 30. They, of a sudden a big shell whizzed by and fell 30 yards to the rear of No 3. The gas alarm was given and I revoked it after making the customary test. More shells 150's and 77's came piling over and it was plain the Germans were out to destroy our guns at any cost - Aggie gave orders to pull out guns' - cease firing and meet me for the engine. George + I ducked four big ones and managed to reach the Motor cycle! Mawhard + Ogive directed the men + the guns were easily pushed to safety - not a man was hit. Direct hits on No 1. dugout - no 2 epi and no 3's trench. I got to engine - found Ogive had taken auto cross country + beat me to it - then I saw the guns come rolling along pushed by the whole battery! Some trucks! I immediately went back to epi, met Aggie en route + was relieved to find him safe, Epis were still being shelled - I found 1 man + sent them down. Came back at 12 with Lieut Howard to check up our projectiles + the blamed Dutchmen repeated this operation - we had to take D

Page from the original Terminal Diary - August 16, 1918

Saturday August 17

Since yesterday, Fritzs had dropped almost 250 big shells on our epis, but our guns are safe – with his usual methods, Fritz is shelling every hour – he is either a fool or we have him fooled.

Ogive has been made orienteer officer for the 53rd C.A.C – his orders to the states have been revoked!

Was rather shocked to find the 1st lines are only 3 ½ kilometers from our epis.

Sunday August 18

Fritz is still firing on us – have established new liaison with French. St. Remy is no more and we are now directly under 21st French Army Corps.

A French propaganda balloon came down near us and I salvaged some literature.

Monday August 19

A full moon brought an air raid on our camp and Suippes – no great harm done.

Another hundred shells fell on our position today. We must have hurt Fritizies feelings – any how he's right mad at us.

Monday August 20

Took the Chaplain (Yates) up to see our guns and position. It was his first visit in the real fighting zone. I prayed for just one shell to come over for excitement's sake but he was duly impressed! French infantry in camp with us have a field day in our honor – races and music etc.

Tuesday August 21

Y.M.C.A entertainer the "St. Louis Four" sang for the men in the battery – pretty good stuff too. For the fifth time in five days I've once more sworn off smoking!

Wednesday August 22

Ordered to fire tomorrow. Went to Châlus to tell Y.M.C.A people we would not have time to listen tonight. We had killed Lillian for the occasion but she proved too tough for comfort. Set up aiming rules after supper. Worked on position until 11 PM – rack to bed. Am doing the orienteer work with transit.

Thursday August 23

[The number "200" is written atop the page]

Up at 5:00 A.M. we "opened up" at 7:08 A.M. not a reply from Fritz. Col. Young and Major Hardaway watched the firing. Results were probably the best we have bad. Very tired but had to return to position at 8:30 P.M. with engine to move guns to "trois bis garage". Was interrupted by order of Col. Young to fire again tomorrow – had to take guns back to position – bed at 1:00 AM.

Friday August 24

Was so tired did not get up until noon. Walt Mac last had gone to Châlus and I took transit to epis. Set up aiming rules.

Was having trouble with the transit. We fire tomorrow if weather permits.

Saturday August 25

We were to fire at 6:30 AM – rose at 4:30 and went to guns – heavy fog and aviator radioed that it was impossible to observe. At ten he reported visibility good and we went back to the guns. Col. Young and Major Hardaway came over at once – and what I expected – happened! Fritz beat us to it this time and before we had fired a shot – the old familiar wha-bang! We did the dugout slide once more. We finally made the fire bus working later. Salvos places our guns under the camouflage and ordered the men back to camp. After this Aggie, Sergeant Nowlin and I left.

Major Hardaway made his gunners slide near when a shell burst over our heads.

After lunch we road back to watch the bombardment – Fritz dropped about 250 of his 150's on our position and tonight he is shelling us again and I cannot bring the engine in to pull off our guns until tomorrow night!

Sunday August 26

Germans shelled epis again las tonight. We have had marvelous luck. Not a gun was destroyed and a dud fell under no. 3 and another under the tool car. Had they exploded – a different story would have been told. I took the guns out tonight and left them in the garage – our movement was watched with interest by a Boche avion but we had to move out regardless. The epis are a literal mess – also the large number of duds laying around is significant of the character of Fritz ammunition.

Monday August 27

Worked all day on transit and geometry, correcting errors in the latter.

The epis were heavily gassed last night – fumes are still very pronounced.

Moved the guns to Trois-bis after 9:00 PM. Nowlin came for me in the car.

Two soldiers carry an aerial bomb, an Austrian dud
that landed nearby but did not explode.

Tuesday August 28

Have had the pip or something all day. Ran a school on the transit for my gun pointers. Held gas drill for the 'H' new men – they have been well trained.

In bed early – feel like a steamed clam.

Wednesday August 29

Telephone drill – gas drill O.D. – and the 'pip' is still with me. This is the life!

Thursday August 30

Four new car loads of ammunition came in – Fritz is making desperate efforts to bring down old '44' the balloon in our camp. The observer had to jump with his parachute twice this afternoon.

Friday August 31

The epis even shelled late this afternoon – I thought I saw gas so I took Serg. Miracle and we went down to see if the guard was O.K. We slipped into the dugouts between salvos and the guard was wearing avmask but found no gas. The shells were falling so fast all around us that we dared not leave and were marooned for two hours – finally we got away between salvos of one minute each – the enemy's fire having shifted a trifle. I had "Chartunsi" with me and the damn coward howled and cried as each shell stuck near our dugout!

10

September

Sunday September 1

Cold drizzle – a hopeless day which makes us long for home.

Inspected new kitchen car.

Aggie has made me signal officer – my "accomplishments" now include – R.R officer – Gas Orienteer and Signal officer – *C'est la guerre.*

Aggie and I rode over to La Cheppe looking for Capt. Vincent and Durandy but they have moved.

Monday September 2

Every artillery was especially active – fired on Suippes, the station and our camp all day – fragments of shell striking around our battery office and shacks. The Y.M.C.A had a narrow escape – as the Doc well knows!

Saw overhead this morning a plucky but one-sided aircraft. Four German planes attacked our friendly balloon – one slow French observation plane went to the defense – the four enemy planes rained bullets on the lone French man who was soon crippled and slowly glided to earth. We ran to its aid and found the pilot's face literally shot off by explosive bullets – he was dead. The observer was unhurt but pitifully reserved by his pilot's death. The plane was demolished but the balloon saved.

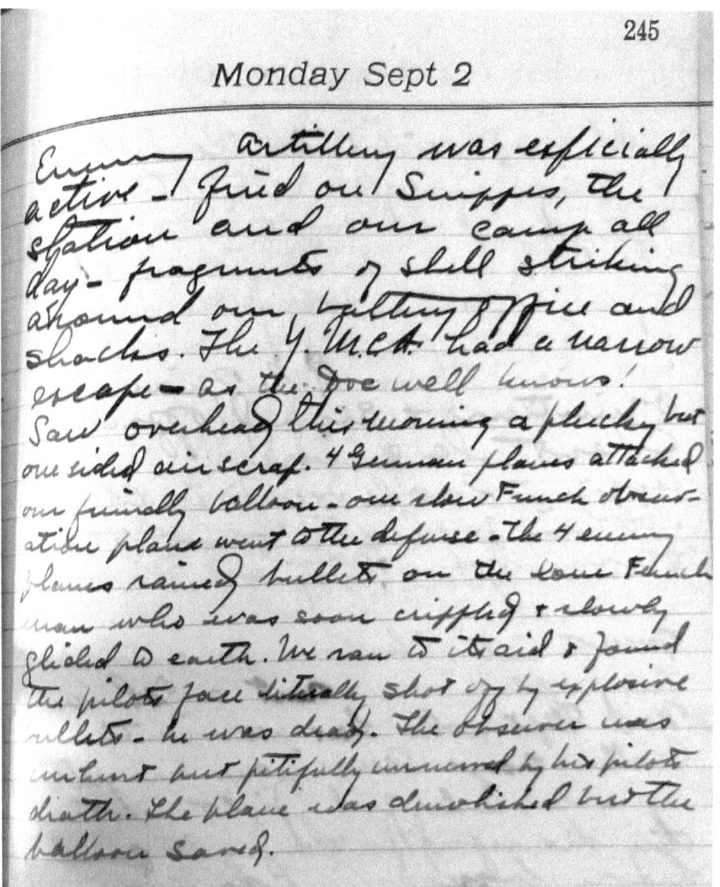

Page out of the original Terminal Diary - September 2, 1918

Tuesday September 3

All last night shells fell into our camp but rather than

spend a cold night in a dugout we took our chances and stuck by our warm beds. Our judgement proved to be splendid!

The epis are again being shelled but every projectile has been a dud. This is remarkable – can it be significant of the character of the Austrians ammunition? Their aim is very accurate.

Went into Châlus for a while this afternoon – met a Col. in Nud. Dept. who has been in the north – says Americans are putting up a wonderful fight but their disregard for danger is causing heavy losses. I dare arranged for a Y.M.C.A performance tomorrow – girls and wow-whee!

Wednesday September 4

Well we had our Y.M.C.A show and it was a peach. We had the ladies and men to dinner – broiled steak, beets, French fries, hot biscuits, coffee, lemon pie – not so bad? One girl played the violin – another sang, another gave a monologue and all were very clever – they will try to come back tomorrow to see our firing position – the girls declare they're not afraid – we'll see!

Oh – Gee – I'll bet they're 118 home sick men in this battery tonight and I'm the biggest baby in the bunch – those blond girls are to blame – wish they would stay home where they belong. We laugh out there but we don't say what we feel like inside.

Thursday September 5

Aggie went into Châlus early this morning and got back the YMCA girls. We took them up to the epis and showed them our battle-scarred position – the Boche was quiet and the girls had a good time – and appropriately wept at the sight of the guard of the Iowa boy which the French had fixed up beautifully – Died on the field of Honor is the inscription.

My order as 1ˢᵗ Lt arrived this morning – I went to Houss-simont and Auve to be sworn in but no Headquarters has a blank oath of office – I'm out of luck for another 24 hours!

The French are going to make a little raid in front of us tonight. It is thought the Boche have retracted and the Frogs are going to find out. *Bonne Chance.*

Friday September 6

Lots of rain today – Badreau came over and swore me in as a 1ˢᵗ Lt – C.A.C. – I am now making a stab for my 1026 francs in back pay but I believe my chances are slim – but what a princely fortune it would be!

Saturday September 7

Aggie and I made a camped inspection of quarters this morning – found the barracks in need of repairs.

There was heavy fighting last night – the French are trying to retake ground lost in July but I do not believe they have been entirely successful.

Sunday September 8

The night fighting continues to be nearby – the Germans have the woods so heavily barbed with entanglements the progress is difficult but the Austrians in the lines are not putting up a very stubborn opposition, but their artillery is excellent.

I took a long walk around the country and found our sector rather uninteresting, not like the old days in July.

Monday September 9

A YMCA physical director came up to camp and I grabbed him – by diplomatic work I got him to secure a swell library for us – 57 books from the Foyer in Suippes. He also gave us a good supply of baseballs etc but the weather is terrific.

Tuesday September 10

Last night's operations grew to the proportions of a battle, but we were not called on – and luckily too as shrapnel in large quantities was dumped on the position.

We are hoping for big things from the American offensive to the South but it is becoming a little late in starting. Rain and high winds are making life miserable for us but the poor fellows in the trenches must be far worse.

Wednesday September 11

The dentist Lt. Seuerlin has arrive much to the discomfort of the men.

More rain, and the wind is blowing a gale. Aggie and I walked to Somme Suippes and back – and got well soaked but got chocolate from the Foyer and a can of anchovies braced us up. After supper we took a hot bath. Aggie is sick tonight – poor soul – I think he wants his Momsey – so do I!

Thursday September 12

Fritz certainly handed us one today – at three o'clock the old familiar whine and bang came over – and we knew we were in for it. Suippes, the station and our camp were shelled all afternoon and to add to our discomfort it rained miserably. At six there was a lull. We ate supper and awaited developments – they came at ten where a shell hit fifty yards from my shacks, blowing up the camp coop. We spent an uncomfortable night in wet muddy dug outs – fighting mosquitos and varmints. At three we couldn't stand it no longer and determined to let the devil take the hindmost – crawled to our beds. I bunked with Walt Mauhart as his shack is fairly well protected. At five, Fritz quit and we slept till nine.

Friday September 13

Things were torn up pretty badly last night but no one

was hurt. Two frogs were sleeping in the coop and the thin cots were flown from under them – they escaped unhurt!

Fritz started again tonight but the French did too. The artillery duel was terrific – we ordered the men to leave camp and sleep by the BC car out of danger – Walt and Doc went too – then Aggie, Sergeants Nowlin and Willet and I kept another Irish wake in the battery office – wondering when the next one would hit and cussing out Fritz but we were all to damn foolish or hard-headed to budge. At one o'clock we voted on sleep – and I took possession of Walt's room and slept despite the noise. We're in a queer situation – we fire – too near the lines for our guns and here we sit in camp like boobs while Fritz took his home. However, he caught his lot tonight.

The American offensive has started on the Lorraine Front – 5 kilometers and 800 prisoners 1st day – yea boa – poor fool Kaiser Bill!

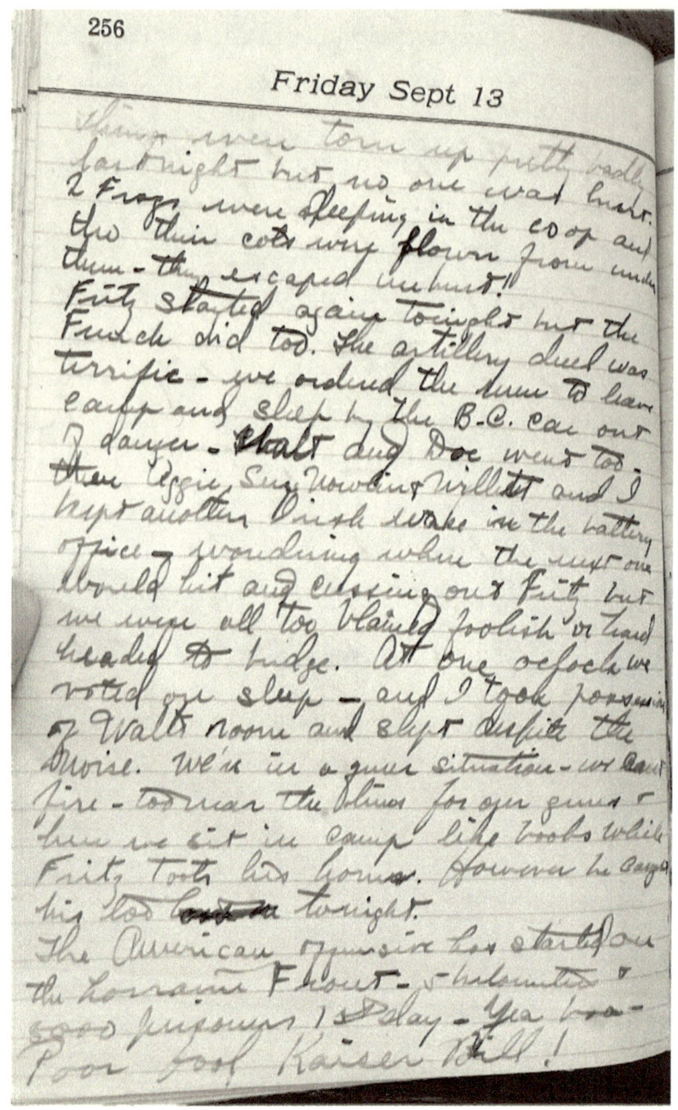

256

Friday Sept 13

Things were torn up pretty badly
last night but no one was hurt.
2 Frogs were sleeping in the coop and
the thin cots were flown from under
them - they escaped unhurt!
Fritz started again tonight but the
French did too. The artillery duel was
terrific - we ordered the men to leave
camp and sleep by the B-C. car out
of danger - Stoalt and Doc went too.
Then Aggie, Suy Nowlin & Willett and I
kept another Irish wake in the battery
office - wondering where the next one
would hit and cussing out Fritz but
we were all too blamed foolish or hard
headed to budge. At one oclock we
voted on sleep - and I took possession
of Walt room and slept despite the
noise. We're in a queer situation - we can't
fire - too near the lines for our guns &
here we sit in camp like boobs while
Fritz toots his horns. However he caught
big too in tonight.
The American offensive has started on
the Lorraine Front - & helmets &
8000 prisoners 1st day - Yea boa -
Poor fool Kaiser Bill!

Page out of the original Terminal Diary - September 13, 1918

Saturday September 14

I booked a ride to Châlus and had a great day. Bought up the town – from live chickens, live lobsters – fresh figs to every kind of fresh vegetable the market affords. Had a fine meal at the Renaud and came home in the car via St. Remy. We passed infantry artillery lines miles long on the national highway – all going out of our sector! When I got back to camp I found Aggie, Srgs. Nowlin and Willet waiting for me, and Fritz had started dropping 'em over as usual. This is getting monotonous to us – wish he would send 'em over in one huge chunk and quit.

The Americans have won a glorious victory at St. Mihiel – gained all our objectives and are resting. France is wild with joy – the arrow in our heart has been removed.

Sunday September 15

We received orders to work today and were in high spirits – we thought we were going to join the Americans – later we learned we would go to Reims. This was naturally good news. Excitement is perpetual on the mountain of Reims. Tonight Major Hardaway phoned the movement had been postponed – I believe there is a shortage of R.R. cars.

Fritz shelled all around us again all night – he is making up a high percentage of duds but is successfully keeping us on the uneasy seat.

We had our "spread" at noon – riz[48] – boiled lobster – cauliflower – fresh tomatoes – French fries – lemonade – and plum pudding. If Fritz knew this wouldn't he be lonesome for peace.

The Lacroix Meuse Fountain. It is now restored and a French landmark in Meuse.

Monday September 16

We scented mischief in the air today – and got it too! At noon the enemy sent over a series of high bursts registering on the station – then dropped one lone shell and all was quiet. Night came and at about 10:30 – whang – bang – and the night began. The second shell hit an ammunition train by the station – never have I witnessed such a terrifying beautiful spectacle. Fourteen rail road cars full of 75's – star shells of all colors and signal rockets blew up – one after the other. It took five hours. The explosions lit up the skies and the shrapnel whistling in continual succession sounded like thousands of guns barfs. Fascinated, we watched the destruction – then Aggie and I slept in Walter's room because it had a good nook. Walt and the Doc had long since pulled out for the B.C. car. I felt pretty safe where I was but I didn't sleep until the worst of the worst was over!

Tuesday September 17

Everything boringly quiet today. I slept until 11:30 despite the continual bursts from the heated shells at the station. In all – 60,000 rounds of ammunition for "75's" was destroyed. I found one whole shell imbedded in the side of my shack this afternoon – 500 yards from the station! The camp is littered with shrapnel.

A French observation plane was shot down over camp this afternoon and fell in almost the identical spot where the last one did. The pilot was killed and observer badly injured.

I played a little ball after supper with Sergeant Davis – then Aggie and I took a hot shower after I had cut my damn head on a low rafter.

Wednesday September 18

Fritz knew he had done things up brown for a while so we slept undisturbed – all the shelling going to our right into Suippes. Nothing of interest has happened – though there is an enormous amount of traffic on the roads at night.

Thursday September 19

Only a few stray big ones came over doing practically no damage and vast stores of ammunition guns and troops have poured into our sector – the truth is – the French are going to make a giant offensive – it will cover an area from Reims to Verdun and will pierce Haunted Hilldenburg line.

I believe we have more artillery with us now than we had in July.

Friday September 20

Damn and then some! Just as we thought we would get into the thick of things we are ordered away – apparently to rest in Haussimont – there of all places. We're going but I can't believe it's Haussimont to rest. Something big is up, we know we are needed here. But what a disappointment to have to leave at this time. The offensive will be wonderful – the amount of material is beyond imagination – millions of shells and hundreds of batteries surround our position – tanks big and small – I can't believe we will have to leave.

"A French observation plane was shot down over
camp this afternoon [...] The pilot was killed." -
September 17, 1918

Saturday September 21

Broke camp this A.M. and retrained during a miserable rain and our spirits pitifully low over having to leave our beloved Front. Everything is ready for the offensive and we are packed off like a bunch of Germans. At St. Hilare we ran into shell fire and it was like taking a cold shower and we all felt better. Aggie had a bad tooth ache and I was up all-night jabbering Frog language for him.

Sunday September 22

We woke up on the garage in Haussimont – and groaned! Detrained in the rain – spent the day orienting ourselves in barracks.

One year ago today, I reported at Fort Monroe for duty – scared as hell!

Monday September 23

We did not have to get up for reveille but were at work on the guns by 8:30 AM.

Our schedule is terrific
5:45 Reveille
6:00-6:15 Physical exercise
7:00 Breakfast
7:40-8:15 Infantry drill
8:30-11:30 Work on guns
1:00 PM to 4:30 lectures instructing the men
5:30-6:00 Retreat and Parade

Our men are thoroughly trained and veterans of the Front and it is a shame to have to treat them like recruits but they are good sports about it.

Tuesday September 24

Aggie is going on permission next Monday – at least he hopes to. Then I'll go when he comes back but we're betting that neither of us gets away nor the other men either. A permission is too vague to be a reality! We put in our 1st day of camp routine today – this reveille business is what ruins the army for me.

Wednesday September 25

More of the old stuff – I've tried to do anything but sleep.

Thursday September 26

Aggie was acting Major today for Parade – oh boy!

I had the battery with Walt. Walt has been made Bn[49] adjutant. I am now senior Lt. in battery. We have one green 2nd Lt. who calls me sir. He has a lot to learn!

Friday September 27

Drill lectures on gas, machine gun, signal instruction in afternoon parade.

Received 1st mail I've had in weeks – feeling more cheerful but the offensive has started and we're eating our hearts out to get into it. We belong on the Front and we know it.

Saturday September 28

Drilled and cleaned guns – Parade is off to Troyes for 2 hours.

Sunday September 29

Beatty and I roamed over Troyes and found our lost Doc. Had a great lunch at the Jeunesse[50] and saw the Petrus[51]. Bought a lot of stuff for the battery and myself. Back to Haussimont at 10:00 P.M.

Monday September 30

Aggie's permission came today – he leaves tomorrow – and I'll be too sorry to think for the next two weeks. The new Lts. know nothing... old routine work.

| 223 |

JOHN LOCKE DOGGETT JR

11

October

Tuesday October 1

Aggie left this morning. I'm too tired to write but I like the job of B.C and can hold it down.

As luck would have it – a request for recommendations from B.Cs on their Lts came in today and since I am the battery commander I couldn't recommend myself! *C'est la guerre.*

Col. Caught Joures and Berdette at Reveille and put them in the guard house. I went to plead their case and got them off with battery punishment – 2 weeks digging after 6:30 PM

Wednesday October 2

Conway, Rivers and Stowes went AWOL and I'm furious. The battery knows it too – I won't stand for anything like this but my sympathy is with the men – the discipline and life here is sickening.

Germany has proposed an armistice. Peace is in the air – I want to go home but let's lick Fritz first. He sees he can't win now and wants to get off easy. Bill Kaiser – you got a spanking coming to you.

Thursday October 3

More peace talks. Major Hardaway and Co. rehashed the 14th offensive and how our artillery in the Champagne won the 2nd battle of the Marne. Those were the days!

I'm too tired for words – I never knew one man could hold down so many jobs at once but I'm doing it and thriving too.

A soldier poses with his armor and weapons,
including a rifle, grenade, and knives.

Friday October 4

More lectures by the Colonel on drills and soldierly bearing!!

Gee – this Haussimont is some hole. Got my rabbit finally located and boarded out for 10 frs a month – also the chicks.

We are camouflaging Chartreuse and Rags. The battery had cabbage for lunch so I ate with their lot. Balled out by the Major on my guard details but I wasn't at fault. Soloed with May: Parade.

Rivers came back and I preferred Chayes vs him immediately.

Saturday October 5

Washed guns with Sal soda – scraped off rust, etc. Battery washed themselves in P.M. I had my school for Lieutenants. Wilson is a good man. Ryan left and Nelson goes soon. De Brie is alright but is almost too quiet.

Sunday October 6

Reveille[52] but no physical exercise – I went back to bed. Kidded the YMCA to sell me 3 cartons of camels for the battery and thus I spent the 20. Mrs. Childs sent me. We parade and ritual in Front of barracks – I forgot to traverse arms! Major Hardaway was away so I didn't catch what I deserved!

Monday October 7

Had all tools cleaned and started painting on guns. Have so many fatigue details out that my battery looks like a pneumonia patient. School with a Major H in P.M. Parade and bed.

Tuesday October 8

Checked tools for No.1 gun – this is a colossal job. Maj. H looked on for a while then quit but made me keep on. However, I learned a lot about what tools we don't need! We stole a bunch of lumber for our barracks. Sergeant Nowlin and I doped out on plans for offices and kitchen – we'll have the best barracks in Haussimont if the Col. don't catch us! School for my Lts. and batting[53] for the battery in P.M. then parade.

Wednesday October 9

We had a very instructive morning – Major Hardaway took the battalion out into the field and we pitched tents and inspected equipment. Worked on barracks in PM, the weather being too cold for athletics. Gave company punishment to 5 men for dirty rifles and lost equipment. We redid the K.P!

Thursday October 10

Cleaned tools on no. 2 guns. Painted some more. Drill – worked on new barracks – now officer's school – Parade and after supper N.C.O.'S school – bed.

Friday October 11

Aggie came back from Paris this morning and took his battery off my hands. I skipped to Mailly to buy a pair of trousers. Missed school but got back for parade. At night Aggie showed me his trophies from Paris – beautiful laces etc for his folks but the pieces were too stiff for me.

Soldiers make a phone call on a field telephone

Saturday October 12

This was proclaimed Liberty Day so all we had to do was rehearse a parade and the ceremony of "Escort to the Colors" which our Battalion was to perform at the afternoon. However, rain prevented and we did not even have retreat. Houras got his 1ˢᵗ Lt and gave a party at officers' mess. I left early to pack up and take a shower for Sunday was to be the day of days!

Sunday October 13

The old darn clock clattered at 5:30 and dragged me cussing from bed to dress in the cold. Aggie chuckling at my discomfiture. However, it was my 1st day of Freedom and I was in good humor as I climbed aboard the mail truck for Somme Sous at 6:10. My train for Troyes was on time and I arrived there at 10:30! I had to spend 7 hours there. Had a fine breakfast at the hotel with 6 eggs confit and coffee.

I walked down to the cathedral and around town to stir up an appetite for lunch. Mailke' Peters and I swapped stories, then I went up and lolled in a tub of hot water. What a luxury!

At the gare I met Lt. Greene of the Engineers and we liked each other – so on reaching Paris we went to the same Hotel Grand International in the Monte Maître. We were late in arriving and after supper fell into bed. But I had 24 hours of Paris ahead! On Permission – I now know why the Frogs get so excited.

Monday October 14

I breakfasted at the lazy hour of 8. Phoned Aunt Claire and arranged for lunch at Premiers. Greene and I went to

Adaous Ex. Co and I drew 1000 francs, giving me 2400[54] in all to blow. By great luck I got a 'bed' in the des Wagon Lits[55] for 78.55 francs! Received mail from home too! We walked around the opera and Place Vendome while I eyed some solitaire rings! At the Continental we took a taxi for Premiers and met Aunt Claire and Uncle Clever – we had a great lunch: lobster – fried oysters and potatoes – coffee – beer – and apricot sherbet all for 94 francs!

After lunch Aunt Claire, Greene and I drove to US Commissary and got some sugar and white bread for Aunt Claire then we got a taxi and drove around Paris for Greene's benefit. The voyage included – Champs Elysee – Arc de Triumph – Eiffel Tower – Tomb des Invalides Place de la Councord – Luxemburg and Sacre Cour. Back to Aunt Claire's for delicious chocolate, hot biscuits and confiture. Greene and I then hiked back to the hotel in time to catch our trains – he to Brittany – I to Nice. I found my stateroom on the train excellent and my roommate a quiet old Frog. We got along famously. I hit the hay at 9 PM.

Tuesday October 15

I woke up dimly aware that I was moving so, so comfortable was my train bed. The old man below was stirring and like all Frogs took his daily 'bath in Perfume. However, Monsieur proved to be an interesting and affable companion.

He knew the country thoroughly and it is due to him that I was able to appreciate the country. At Aurières we breakfasted on wonderful grapes and a new sort of fruit – coffee and ham sandwiches! En route he showed me the old castles of the 14th and 15th centuries where the Pope lived, gloriously preserved old fortresses. Then came a vast wilderness where the sea had receded. Next, the mountains – far away, they were a hazy blue – but soon became a wonderful deep green studded with olive groves – grape vines – and vegetables. We neared Marseille and I got my first glimpse of the Rhine and the chateaus on high cliffs – then the Mediterranean – bluest of blue in color and the high shores a ruddy red. I spent the hour in Marseille full of people of every nationality. Then for 8 hours the train skirted the sea – Never have I seen greater beauty. Snow topped mountains – the sea – white mansions and red tile; Palau trees – cypress – olive and pine. Past salt workers and into Nice. Registered at PM and got a room at the Luxemburg[56]. My room overlooks the sea – the roar of the wave reminds me of Atlantic beach. Oh – how I wish for the beaches. I'm off to sleep with a new love for France.

Winston Churchill[57] and I ate dinner at the same table.

288

Tuesday Oct 15

I woke up dimly aware that I was moving
so comfortable was my train bed. The old man
below was stirring + like all Frogs took his daily
bath in Perfume. However Monsieur proved to
be an interesting + affable companion. He knew
the country thoroughly + it is due to him that I was
able to appreciate the country. At Avignon we breakfasted
on wonderful grapes + an new sort of fruit - coffee +
ham sandwiches! En route he showed me the old
castles of the 14th + 15th centuries when the Pope
lived - gloriously preserved old fortresses. Then
came a vast wilderness where the sea had receded. Next
the mountains. far away they were a hazy blue - but soon
became a wonderful deep green studded with olive
groves - grape vines - and vegetables. We neared Marseilles
+ I got my first glimpse of the Rhone + the chateaus on
high cliffs - then the Mediterranean - blue + of blue in color
+ the high shores a ruddy red. I spent one hour in Marseilles
full of people of conversationally. Then for 8 hours the train skirted
the sea - now have I seen greater beauty, snow topped
mountains - the sea - white mansions + red tile; Palm
trees - bananas - cypress - olive + pine. Past salt works
+ into Nice. Registered at P.M + got a room at the Luxemburg
my room overlooks the sea - the roar of the waves reminds me of Atlantic beach. oh- how I wish for the
folks. I'm going to sleep with a new love for France.
Winston Churchill + late dinner at the same table

Page out of the original Terminal Diary - October 15,
1918

Wednesday October 16

At Reveille hour I was awake but instead of seeing the dirty mud holes of Haussimont outside – I found my room flooded with sunlight. The Mediterranean shore is like a turquoise. I lolled in my luxury and went back to sleep! Later had breakfast served in bed and got up in time for lunch. Walked around Nice – met Capt. Briggs and we joined forces. Took in a concert at the Casino at night. We are going to Monte Carlo tomorrow.

Thursday October 17

Up at 6:15 for breakfast. We caught 7 AM tramway for Monaco and made for 1 ½ hour along the coast between the mountains and the sea. The fastest ride I've ever had. Saw 6 water spouts. At Monte Carlo we went to the casino – the gambling rooms, ball rooms, and opera. Went to the museum where the Prince's trophies are preserved from his fishing expeditions. Saw his Palace. Had lunch at the Carlton where Charlie, a Norfolk negro, reigns supreme. Took a tramway for Manitou – then back into Italy – on the frontier we sent Port Cards home. Returned to Nice by train in time for supper. Went to the Casino at night.

Friday October 18

Encore breakfast in bed – then went shopping – did all my Santy Claus but wished I had enough to buy up the town. Went to concert again at night.

Saturday October 19

Took a swim in the nude – it was great. Took a drive around town – into the L'église russe[58] etc. Had tea at YMCA as we are shut out of the casino on account of Grippe.

Sunday October 20

Took tramway for Monte Carlo – we had lunch again at Carlton – pigeons and partridges and mushrooms! Went to a wonderful concert in the opera house – stayed in Monte Carlo for supper and rode back to Nice by moonlight – the trip was too beautiful to describe and I got homesick as a baby – I'll bet Momsey and Louise know why.

Monday October 21

Rain this morning did not prevent me from taking a good

swim – though I confess it took courage to leave my good old bed.

Capt. Briggs and I went on another shopping expedition. I think I'm a sucker or Marcelle is a clever sales lady. Anyhow she, the Madame and ugly sister, are going to dinner with Captains Briggs and McGee at the Negresco Hotel.

Talked to some Red Cross nurse and then wrote a letter.

Tuesday October 22

Rain again and now I cannot visit Grasse – I'm broke any way.

Bummed around Nice for the last time.
The Madame and Co. dined with us in style – Celery soup, lobsters, roast chicken (ah!), fried spuds, *haricots verts*, salad, coffee, *fromage* – afterwards we took a ride along the shore in moonlight and Madame sang beautifully – Made me have some of that "I want to go home" feeling – so I wrote to Reddie.

Wednesday October 23

I said Au Revoir to Nice and my friends at 11:36 AM.

Travelled all day and slept sitting up like a Central Park Monk because a big Frenchie Dame next to me had a hair lip and "slept" through her mouth – some vocal expert but hardly a nightingale.

Thursday October 24

Arrived Paris at 1030. Got a seven-hour extension and so don't leave until 5pm tomorrow. Went to Grand Hotel International– shaved up, phoned Aunt Claire without success. Had lunch at Premiers! Spent afternoon getting packages off and went to Commissary for smokes and sugar. Finally got Aunt Claire – she has grippe – fever is in town. Went to University Union and was told of Red's death – cannot believe Red has been killed – I went back to my Hotel as I would not or did not now feel like seeing any one. Oh – these dammed Huns.

Friday October 25

I spent the morning with Aunt Claire – she is pretty sick. Tried once more to get Gabardine for Louise – Aunt Claire is going to look at the samples for me. Met Greene and Mrs Wittenby at Hotel Lotti[59] – we had lunch at Chinese Mubella – Greene is love sick and I felt too rotten to talk. Went to Rue

St. Anne and the Doctor[60] said I could stay in Paris if I went to hospital – but I went to Gare du Nord and bought a ticket on 8 PM train to Châlus and the M.P. extended my ticket three hours. I went back to Aunt Claire's for tea – met Greene and his girl at 8 o'clock for Châlus. Stayed there 'till 4:26 AM.

I'll never forget how beautiful Paris was in her gala attire in ru Lille.

Saturday October 26

Arrived Somme-Sous at 6:30 AM and booked a ride to camp on the mail jitney. Slept all morning but I went on duty at noon. The battery is the same but we lost 20 men in the hospital with the flu. I am feeling rotten myself – have had two chills. The Captain is sick too

I have been commissioned one year today.

Sunday October 27

Recall sounded at Reveille so I slept on – am feeling better and Major Hardaway and Capt. Hazleton are ordered to Front for observation with the 14" Naval guns – Aggie is acting Major and I am taking over the Battery again.

Soldiers eat and rest together as the war draws to an end

Monday October 28

Spent the morning moving our guns around so the 73rd and 74th can train on there. This is a mess – we have just repainted everything and now a bunch of recruits will spill the beans.

Leveled barracks this PM. Our one quarters are OK but the ficus rooms are mere pigeon holes.

Tuesday October 29

Capt. Garduier is rich abed. Walter is acting Major and I am enjoying myself as Battery Boss.

There are more rumors about us driving over 14" guns[61] – but Austria is begging for Peace again. I believe the war is over – but I want another chance at the Germans for what they did to Red – Col. Guis ordered us to instruct the 74 on our guns and I was detailed as instructor – fat job – we never had anyone to instruct us.

Wednesday October 30

Inspection this AM then I took 11:30 jitney for Mailly – saw Greene and I had lunch with him – that boy is so love sick it's pitiful. I am too but I'm not pitiful – at least I don't spread my sorrows.

Aggie is up today and we battle tonight – as usual it's a solemn occasion.

Thursday October 31

Spent the day instructing the 73rd at the epis – it's not my job either – but then it's all in the Army.

JOHN LOCKE DOGGETT JR

12

November

Friday November 1

Pay day! But it don't do me any good – I owe the whole damn business to Aggie and then some – Nice was nice but – costly! Down to guns in AM – took a hike in PM.

Saturday November 2

I think I'm going to rot in this joint – I didn't even enjoy rabbit tonight. Haussimont would ruin the morale of Angels – rain, wind, cold – and doing nothing of any practical value.

Sunday November 3

Aggie went to Troyes last night to see the Petrus. I played around here and watched the clock – I wonder how long Fritz can stand the pressure. We'd give six months pay for another shot at him.

Monday November 4

Major Hardaway and Capt. Hazleton came back from the Front with big dope – we are all to get 14 inch naval guns, the biggest guns we have! This is quite an honor to the battalion as only a few of these big guns are in France and we are amongst the chosen few.

Tuesday November 5

Battery went on guard and I'm Officer of the Day for the camp – a sweet task – ah! Oui! Have inspected two reliefs – the last at 1:00 AM while the rain and wind lived up to their old habits.

Wednesday November 6

Relieved of O.D at 3:30 – all prisoners safe – and I didn't get balled out – now I'm going to knock off a few hours' sleep!

Doc Chapman got his captaincy and gave us a party at the news

Thursday November 7

Sad – sad day – Aggie is ordered to report to take command of Battery D of the 52nd – Capt. Gilmore is assigned to our battery, so I'm out of luck. Never felt lower – my only hope is that our 14-inch guns come up soon – we are to have 2, and battery F to have one. I'd welcome a pop gun to get out of here and back on the Front.

Rags was killed this morning – everything is going wrong except the war.

Friday November 8

Aggie left this morning but Great Scott – I'm dizzy – I

have been promoted to captaincy and ORDERED HOME –
oh Gee – I can't believe it all. Somebody is mighty generous –
I'm too full for utterance tonight.

I stood retreat for the last time with the Battery – I feel
queer about this going Home – my house is there but every
man in the battery is my friend – we soldiered this exciting
time and I ought to stay here – however I have no decision
in the matter – orders are orders – and that Christmas dinner
will have to be a big one!

Was sworn in as Capt. this afternoon – and have my party
tonight.

Saturday November 9

Went to Mailly and cabbed home – I'm broke but think
my credit will get me to Paris – also Father is coming to
the rescue!

Moved over all battery accounts to Wilson – the poor boy
is blue – but I'm in the skies though I can't believe it yet.
At Mailly I found I would have been put in command of the
battery to take it to the Front with the 14's – now instead –
goodnight!

Sunday November 10

Am all packed up – ready but RAR Headquarters say "hold fast until further orders". I'll never believe I'm going home until I start for Paris. We think everything depends on whether Germany accepts the Armistice or not. The Kaiser has abdicated so I might as well start having my spuds! Everyone in the Battalion is nervous of us lucky ones - Capt. Hazleton, Capt. Mauhart and Mister Mess – Gosh – I've fooled some of the people anyway!

Monday November 11

The Armistice was signed this morning officially – I can scarcely believe that the end came – we got our clearance papers and left for Paris via Troyes. Arrived Paris 10:30 and the town was wild. Thousands filled the streets - singing, cheering, kissing every American, and parading with flags of all the allies. Hazleton and I went up town at midnight and stopped at Place de l'Opera where a huge crowd had gathered to sing, make speeches. Paris is mad with joy and is celebrating as only Paris can.

Tuesday November 12

Walter and I started out in the morning for Adeus Ex. Where I casted a draft on Father for 200 bucks[62], poor Father! I went to A.P.M and got our extension of 24 hours in Paris. Lunch at Premiers with Hazleton and after dinner I met Walt and we went to Gau d'Est for our baggage – we had to fight our way through the crowds – parades after parades of cheering girls, soldiers and Parisians – as stores closed. Got our baggage off and went to Place de la Concorde – here the square was a swelling mass of wild people dragging captured German couriers through the streets. Pictures of Kaiser and Co in ludicrous poses. At Hotel Continental I phoned Aunt Claire and we went up to see her for tea. The mob spirit caught me and I joined in the parades at night.

Wednesday November 13

This morning I met Aunt Claire and we went shopping – finally found some blue cloth for Louise and brought some blouses for Momsey and the girls.

Packed up after lunch and beat it for the train which we took as Gaumont passed into Brest.

Thursday November 14

Arrived in Brest – a dirty but interesting seaport in Brittany.

Am signed up and waiting for transportation home – as excited as a two-year-old.

Had a good bath!

Cover of the original Terminal Diary

Epilogue

After returning home, John Locke Doggett Jr. worked as a lawyer, married Miriam Lee Jones, and fathered two daughters, Nancy and Miriam. A successful business and family man - still, John suffered from a disease that did not officially exist yet – post-traumatic stress disorder - and being unable to escape the grip of the Great War, on March 17th 1959 he took his own life.

"We laugh out here but we don't say what we feel like inside" - September 4, 1918

John and his wife, Miriam in the 1940s

Endnotes

Endnotes

1. Fort Monroe: Active from 1834 till the Operational Armament was removed (after World War II). Located in Hampton, Virginia.
2. Fort Screven: Active Military Base used in the Spanish-American War, World War I, and World War II, located on Tybee Island, Georgia. Named after Revolutionary War hero, General Joseph Screven.
3. influenza
4. vomited
5. SS Philedelphia
6. Reference to Lilliput, the village of tiny people of Gulliver's Travels
7. shillings
8. reference to the typified "rags-to-riches" story
9. A city of northeast France on the Seine River east-southeast of Paris. A pre-Roman town, it was a prosperous commercial center in the Middle Ages and was noted for its annual fairs, which set standards of weights and measures for all of Europe.
10. A river, about 523 km (325 mi) long, of northeast France flowing generally northwest to the Seine River
11. A river of northeast France flowing about 225 km (140 mi) to the Seine River north-northwest of Troyes.
12. Slang term for French soldier – reference to the thick mustache and beard typical of French Soldiers
13. French for "soldier"

14. A soldier assigned to attend and perform various tasks for a superior officer

15. Reddie was a serious love interest of John

16. Vitry-en-Artois

17. "French for "afternoon"

18. Donac is a small saltwater clam found in Jacksonville FL, Doggetts hometown

19. A simple mortar-like weapon that could throw large drums filled with flammable or toxic chemicals

20. 3-inch trench mortar is a smooth-bore, muzzle-loading weapon for high angles of fire. Although it is called a 3-inch mortar, its bore is actually 3.2 inches or 81 mm

21. An epis is a curved track

22. To sleep soundly, to rest deeply

23. Quoits is a traditional game which involves the throwing of rings over a set distance, usually to land over a spike.

24. French for "new'

25. Mustard gas or Sulphur mustard

26. A military officer who acts as an administrative assistant to a senior officer

27. Watchmen

28. The French Air Force unit escadrille N 124 during the First World War

29. A military decoration of France awarded for acts of heroism in combat

30. Slang term referring to Austrians

31. Portuguese

32. A salvo is the simultaneous discharge of artillery or firearms including the firing of guns either to hit a target or to perform a salute.

33. Railroad

34. French for "its quite good"

35. James Reese Europe of the 369th Regimental Band, also known as the Harlem Hellfighters, a band that helped initiate the Harlem Renaissance.

36. Jazz music

37. Note a typo – clearly says JA. M but meaning is uncertain

38.   This is likely incorrect spelling

39.   The small box respirator was the initial compact version of the recent gas mask.

40.   This is the Second Battle of the Marne, which was the last major German offensive on the Western Front during the First World War. The attack failed when an Allied counterattack, supported by several hundred tanks, overwhelmed the Germans on their right flank, inflicting severe casualties. The German defeat marked the start of the relentless Allied advance which culminated in the Armistice with Germany about 100 days later.

41.   A boy employed on a sailing warship to carry powder to the guns.

42.   The Akron-Tissot gas mask

43.   Clean or brighten the surface of (something)

44.   Distinguished Service Cross

45.   A commune in the Marne department in northeastern France.

46.   French for "right away"

47.   French slang word, used colloquially it is an insult expressing that someone is a jerk or moron

48.   French for "rice"

49.   Bn means battalion

50.   Institut Mondial d'Art de la Jeunesse – UNESCO heritage cultural site

51.   In the Troyes Cathedral, it is either: a heavy bells which made a deep note, for tolling on solemn occasions. OR a stained glass window depicting St. Petrus

52.   A signal to get up in the morning

53.   A batman is a soldier or airman assigned to a commissioned officer as a personal servant. The action of serving as a batman was referred to as "batting".

54.   About $8600 USD today

55.   Compagnie Internationale des Wagons-Lits – Luxury wagon particularly known for its on-train catering and sleeping car services, as well as being the historical operator of the *Orient Express*.

56.   "Apartment Royal Luxembourg Promenade Anglais – Nice" It still exists today

57.   At the time, he was a member of British Parliament and the Minister of Munitions
58.   Orthodox church in Monte Carlo
59.   7 Rue de Castiglione, 75001 Paris, France
60.   Sainte Anne Hospital Center, 14th arrondissement of Paris
61.   14"/50 caliber railway guns
62.   About $3,641

About the Editor

Gabrielle Rose Barbour is the great-granddaughter of your author, John Locke Doggett Jr and is from Long Island, New York. Barbour obtained a masters degree in Arabic and International Affairs before deciding on a career change and returning to school to study astrophysics at Columbia University. She now lives and works in Philadelphia as an aerospace engineer.

Her life's goal is to build a two-story library in her home and maintain a small farm in Pennsylvania.